ROLLO
IN ROME

JACOB ABBOTT

1st WORLD
LIBRARY
Literary Society

Rollo in Rome

Jacob Abbott

© 1st World Library, 2009
PO Box 2211
Fairfield, IA 52556
www.1stworldlibrary.com
First Edition

LCCN: 2009923402

Softcover ISBN: 978-1-4218-8853-8
Hardcover ISBN: 978-1-4218-8952-8
eBook ISBN: 978-1-4218-8754-8

Purchase *"Rollo in Rome"*
as a traditional bound book at:
www.1stWorldLibrary.com/purchase.asp?ISBN=978-1-4218-8853-8

1st World Library is a literary, educational organization
dedicated to:

- Creating a free internet library of downloadable ebooks

- Hosting writing competitions and offering book
publishing scholarships.

Interested in more 1st World Library books?
contact: literacy@1stworldlibrary.com
Check us out at: www.1stworldlibrary.com

1st World Library Literary Society

Giving Back to the World

"If you want to work on the core problem, it's early school literacy."

- James Barksdale, former CEO of Netscape

"No skill is more crucial to the future of a child, or to a democratic and prosperous society, than literacy."

- Los Angeles Times

"Literacy... means far more than learning how to read and write... The aim is to transmit... knowledge and promote social participation."

- UNESCO

"Literacy is not a luxury, it is a right and a responsibility. If our world is to meet the challenges of the twenty-first century we must harness the energy and creativity of all our citizens."

- President Bill Clinton

"Parents should be encouraged to read to their children, and teachers should be equipped with all available techniques for teaching literacy, so the varying needs and capacities of individual kids can be taken into account."

- Hugh Mackay

CONTENTS

CHAPTER I

THE DILIGENCE OFFICE

Rollo went to Rome in company with his uncle George, from Naples. They went by the diligence, which is a species of stage coach. There are different kinds of public coaches that ply on the great thoroughfares in Italy, to take passengers for hire; but the most common kind is the diligence.

The diligences in France are very large, and are divided into different compartments, with a different price for each. There are usually three compartments below and one above. In the Italian diligences, however, or at least in the one in which Mr. George and Rollo travelled to Rome, there were only three. First there was the *interior*, or the body of the coach proper. Directly before this was a compartment, with a glass front, containing one seat only, which looked forward; there were, of course, places for three persons on this seat. This front compartment is called the *coupe*.[1] It is considered the best in the diligence.

[Footnote 1: Pronounced *coupay*.]

There is also a seat up above the *coupe*, in a sort of

second story, as it were; and this was the seat which Mr. George and Rollo usually preferred, because it was up high, where they could see better. But for the present journey Mr. George thought the high seat, which is called the *banquette*, would not be quite safe; for though it was covered above with a sort of chaise top, still it was open in front, and thus more exposed to the night air. In ordinary cases he would not have been at all afraid of the night air, but the country between Naples and Rome, and indeed the country all about Rome, in every direction, is very unhealthy. So unhealthy is it, in fact, that in certain seasons of the year it is almost uninhabitable; and it is in all seasons considered unsafe for strangers to pass through in the night, unless they are well protected.

There is, in particular, one tract, called the *Pontine Marshes*, where the road, with a sluggish canal by the side of it, runs in a straight line and on a dead level for about twenty miles. It so happened that in going to Rome by the diligence, it would be necessary to cross these marshes in the night, and this was an additional reason why Mr. George thought it better that he and Rollo should take seats inside.

The whole business of travelling by diligence in Europe is managed in a very different way from stage coach travelling in America. You must engage your place several days beforehand; and when you engage it you have a printed receipt given you, specifying the particular seats which you have taken, and also containing, on the back of it, all the rules and regulations of the service. The different seats in the several compartments of the coach are numbered, and the prices of them are different. Rollo went so early to engage the passage for himself and Mr. George that he had his choice of all the seats. He took Nos. 1 and 2 of the *coupe*. He paid the money and took the receipt. When he got home, he sat down by the window, while Mr. George was finishing his breakfast, and amused himself by studying out the rules and regulations printed on the back of his ticket. Of course they were in Italian; but Rollo found that he could understand them very well.

"If we are not there at the time when the diligence starts, we lose our money, uncle George," said he. "It says here that they won't pay it back again."

"That is reasonable," said Mr. George. "It will be our fault if we are not there."

"Or our misfortune," said Rollo; "something might happen to us."

"True," said Mr. George; "but the happening, whatever it might be, would be *our* misfortune, and not theirs, and so we ought to bear the loss of it."

"If the baggage weighs more than thirty *rotolos*, we must pay extra for it," continued Rollo. "How much is a *rotolo*, uncle George?"

"I don't know," said Mr. George, "but we have so little baggage that I am sure we cannot exceed the allowance."

"The baggage must be at the office two hours before the time for the diligence to set out," continued Rollo, passing to the next regulation on his paper.

"What is that for?" asked Mr. George.

"So that they may have time to load it on the carriage, they say," said Rollo.

"Very well," said Mr. George, "you can take it to the office the night before."

"They don't take the risk of the baggage," said Rollo, "or at least they don't guarantee it, they say, against unavoidable accidents or superior force. What does that mean?"

"Why, in case the diligence is struck by lightning, and our trunk is burned up," replied Mr. George, "or in case it is attacked by robbers, and carried away, they don't undertake to pay the damage."

"And in case of *smarrimento*," continued Rollo, "they say they won't pay damages to the amount of more than nine dollars, and so forth; what is a *smarrimento*, uncle George?"

"I don't know," said Mr. George.

"It may mean a smash-up," said Rollo.

"Very likely," said Mr. George.

"Every traveller," continued Rollo, looking again at his paper, "is responsible, personally, for all violations of the custom-house regulations, or those of the police."

"That's all right," said Mr. George.

"And the last regulation is," said Rollo, "that the travellers cannot smoke in the diligence, nor take any dogs in."

"Very well," said Mr. George, "we have no dogs, and we don't wish to smoke, either in the diligence or any where else."

Jacob Abbott

"They are very good regulations," said Rollo; and so saying, he folded up the paper, and put it back into his wallet.

On the evening before the day appointed for the journey, Rollo took the valise which contained the principal portion of his own and his uncle's clothes, and went with it in a carriage to the office. Mr. George offered to accompany him, but Rollo said it was not necessary, and so he took with him a boy named Cyrus, whom he had become acquainted with at the hotel.

The carriage, when it arrived at the diligence station, drove in under an archway, and entered a spacious court surrounded by lofty buildings. There was a piazza, with columns, all around the court. Along this piazza, on the four sides of the building, were the various offices of the different lines of diligences, with the diligences themselves standing before the doors.

"Now, Cyrus," said Rollo, "we have got to find out which is our office."

But Rollo was saved any trouble on this score, for the coachman drove the carriage directly to the door of the office for Rome. Rollo had told him that that was his destination, before leaving the hotel.

There was a man in a sort of uniform at the door of the office. Rollo pointed to his valise, and said, in Italian, "For Rome to-morrow morning." The man said, "Very well," and taking the valise out of the carriage, he put it in the office. Then Rollo and Cyrus got into the carriage again, and rode away.

The next morning Mr. George and Rollo went down to

breakfast before six o'clock. While they were eating their breakfast, the waiter came in with a cold roast chicken upon a plate, which he set down upon the table.

"Ah!" said Mr. George, "that is for us to eat on the way."

"Don't the diligence stop somewhere for us to dine?" asked Rollo.

"Yes," said Mr. George, "I presume it stops for us to dine, but as we are going to be out all night, I thought perhaps that we might want a supper towards morning. Besides, having a supper will help keep us awake in going across the Pontine Marshes."

"Must we keep awake?" asked Rollo.

"So they say," replied Mr. George. "They say you are more likely to catch the fever while you are asleep than while you are awake."

"I don't see why we should be," said Rollo.

"Nor do I," said Mr. George.

If Mr. George really did not know or understand a thing, he never pretended to know or understand it.

"It may be a mere notion," said Mr. George, "but it is a very prevailing one, at any rate; so I thought it would be well enough for us to have something to keep us awake."

"We will take some bread and butter too," said Rollo.

Mr. George said that that would be an excellent plan. So they each of them cut one of the breakfast rolls which were on the table in two, and after spreading the inside surfaces well with butter, they put the parts together again. The waiter brought them a quantity of clean wrapping paper, and with this they wrapped up both the chicken and the rolls, and Rollo put the three parcels into his bag.

"And now," said Rollo, "what are we to do for drink?"

"We might take some oranges," suggested Mr. George.

"So we will," said Rollo. "I will go out into the square and buy some."

Rollo, accordingly, went out into the square, and for what was equivalent to three cents of American money he bought six oranges. He put the oranges into his pockets, and returned to the hotel.

He found Mr. George filling a flat bottle with coffee. He had poured some coffee out of the coffee pot into the pitcher of hot milk, which had still a considerable quantity of hot milk remaining in it, and then, after putting some sugar into it, and waiting for the sugar to dissolve, he had commenced pouring it into the flat bottle.

"We may like a little coffee too," said Mr. George, "as well as the oranges. We can drink it out of my drinking cup."

Rollo put his oranges into Mr. George's bag, for his own bag was now full. When all was ready, and the hotel bill was paid, Mr. George and Rollo got into a carriage which the waiter had sent for to come to the door, and set off for the diligence office. It was only half past seven when they arrived there. Rollo saw what time it was by the great clock which was put up on the front of one of the buildings towards the court yard.

"We are too early by half an hour," said Rollo.

"Yes," said Mr. George, "in travelling over new ground we must always plan to be too early, or we run great risk of being too late."

"Never mind," said Rollo, "I am glad that we are here before the time, for now I can go around and see the other diligences getting ready to go off."

So Rollo began to walk about under the portico, or piazza, to the various diligences which were getting ready to set out on the different roads. There was one where there was a gentleman and two ladies who were quite in trouble. I suppose that among the girls who may read this book there may be many who may think that it must necessarily be a very agreeable thing to travel about Europe, and that if they could only go,—no matter under what circumstances,—they should experience an almost uninterrupted succession of pleasing sensations. But the truth is, that travelling in Europe, like every other earthly source of pleasure, is very far from being sufficient of itself to confer happiness. Indeed, under almost all the ordinary circumstances in which parties of travellers are placed, the question whether they are to enjoy themselves and be happy on any particular day of their journey, or to be discontented and miserable, depends so much upon little things which they did not at all take into the account, or even foresee at all in planning the journey, that it is wholly uncertain when you look upon a party of travellers that you meet on the road, whether they are really having a good time or not. You cannot tell at all by the outward circumstances.

There was a striking illustration of this in the case of the party that attracted Rollo's attention in the court of the diligence office. The gentleman's name was Howland. One of the ladies was his young wife, and the other lady was her sister. The sister's name was Louise. Mr. Howland intended to have taken the whole *coupe* for his party; but when he went to the office, the day before, to take the places, he found that one of the seats of the *coupe* had been engaged by a gentleman who was travelling alone.

"How unlucky!" said Mr. Howland to himself. "We must have three seats, and it won't do for us to be shut up in the interior, for there we cannot see the scenery at all."

So he went home, and asked his wife what it would be best to do. "We cannot have three seats together," said he, "unless we go up upon the *banquette*."

But the bride said that she could not possibly ride on the *banquette*. She could not climb up to such a high place.

Now, Mrs. Howland's real reason for not being willing to ride on the banquette, was not the difficulty of climbing up, for at all the diligence offices they have convenient step ladders for the use of the passengers in getting up and down. The real reason was, she thought it was not genteel to ride there. And in fact it is not genteel. There is no part of the diligence where people who attach much importance to the fashion of the thing are willing to go, except the coupe.

"And we don't want to ride in the interior," said Mr. Howland.

"No," said the bride, "that is worse than the banquette."

"Nor to wait till another day," added Mr. Howland.

"No," said Mrs. Howland. "We must go to-morrow, and we must have the *coupe*. The gentleman who has engaged the third seat will give it up to us, I am sure, when he knows that it is to oblige a lady. You can engage the two seats in the coupe, and one more, either on the banquette or in the interior, and then when the time comes to set out we will get the gentleman to let us have his seat. You can pay him the difference."

"But, Angelina," said Mr. Howland, "I should not like to ask such a thing of the gentleman. He has taken pains to go a day or two beforehand to engage his seat, so as to make sure of a good one, and I don't think we ought to expect him to give it up to accommodate strangers."

"O, he won't mind," said Mrs. Howland. "He would as lief change as not. And if he won't, we can arrange it in some way or other."

So Mr. Howland engaged the two places in the coupe, and one on the banquette. When the morning came, he brought his two ladies to the diligence station in good season. He was very unwilling to ask the gentleman to give up his seat; but his wife, who was a good deal accustomed to have her own way, and who, besides, being now a bride, considered herself specially entitled to indulgences, declared that if her husband did not ask the gentleman, she would ask him herself.

"Very well," said Mr. Howland, "I will ask him then."

So Mr. Howland went to the gentleman, and asked him. He was standing at the time, with his umbrella and walking stick in his hand, near one of the pillars of the

Jacob Abbott

portico, smoking a cigar. He looked at Mr. Howland with an expression of some surprise upon his countenance on hearing the proposition, took one or two puffs from his cigar before replying, and then said quietly that he preferred the seat that he had taken in the coupe.

"It would be a very great favor to us, if you would exchange with us," said Mrs. Howland, who had come up with her husband, and stood near. "We are three, and we want very much to be seated together. We will very gladly pay the difference of the fare."

The gentleman immediately, on being thus addressed by Mrs. Howland, took the cigar out of his mouth, raised his hat, and bowed very politely.

"Are you and this other lady the gentleman's party?" he asked.

"Yes, sir," said Mrs. Howland.

"Then I cannot possibly think of giving up my seat in the coupe," replied the gentleman. "I am a Russian, it is true, but I am not a bear, as I should very justly be considered, if I were to leave a compartment in the coach when *two* such beautiful ladies as you were coming into it, especially under the influence of any such consideration as that of saving the difference in the fare."

The gentleman said this in so frank and good-natured a way that it was impossible to take offence at it, though Mr. Howland felt, that by making the request and receiving such a reply, he had placed himself in a very ridiculous position.

"I prize my seat more than ever," said the Russian, still

addressing the ladies; "I prize it incalculably, and so I cannot think of going up upon the banquette. But if the gentleman will go up there, I will promise to take the very best care of the ladies possible, while they are in the coupe."

Mrs. Howland then took Louise aside, and asked, in a whisper, whether she should have any objection to ride in the interior, in case Mr. Howland could exchange the place on the banquette for one within. Louise was quite troubled that her sister should make such a proposal. She said she should not like very well to go in there among so many strangers, and in a place, too, where she could not see the scenery at all. Besides, Louise thought that it would have been more generous in Angelina, if she thought it necessary for one or the other of them to ride inside, to have offered to take a seat there herself, instead of putting it off upon her sister, especially since it was not so proper, she thought, for her, being a young lady, to ride among strangers, as for one who was married.

Mr. Howland then suggested that they should all ascend to the banquette. The persons who had the other two seats there would of course be willing to change for the coupe; or at least, since the coupe was considered the best place, there would be no indelicacy in asking them to do it.

But the bride would not listen to this proposal. She never could climb up there, in the world, she said.

By this time the coach was ready, and the conductor began to call upon the passengers to take their places, so that there was no more time for deliberation. They were all obliged to take their seats as the conductor called off the names from his way bill. The two ladies entered the coupe in company with the Russian, while Mr. Howland ascended by the step ladder to his seat on the banquette. While the passengers were thus getting seated the postilions were putting in the horses, and in a moment more the diligence set off.

Now, here were four persons setting out on a pleasant morning, in a good carriage, to take the drive from Naples to Rome—one of the most charming drives that the whole tour of Europe affords, and yet not one of them was in a condition to enjoy it. Every one was dissatisfied, out of humor, and unhappy. The Russian gentleman was displeased with Mr. Howland for asking him to give up his seat, and he felt uncomfortable and ill at ease in being shut up with two ladies, who he knew were displeased with him for not giving it up. The bride was vexed with the Russian for insisting on his place in the coupe, and with her sister for not being willing to go into the interior, so that she might ride with her husband. Miss Louise was offended at having been asked to sit in the interior, which request, she said to herself, was only part of a systematic plan, which her sister seemed to have adopted for the whole journey, to make herself the principal personage in every thing, and to treat her, Louise, as if she was of no consequence whatever. And last of all, Mr. Howland, on the banquette above, was out of humor with himself for having asked the Russian to give up his seat, and thus subjected himself to the mortification of a refusal, and with his wife for having required him to ask it.

Thus they were all at heart uncomfortable and unhappy, and as the horses trotted swiftly on along the smooth and beautiful road which traverses the rich campagna of Naples, on the way to Capua, the splendid scenery was wholly disregarded by every one of them.

Now, it is very often so with parties travelling in Europe.

The external circumstances are all perhaps extremely favorable, and they are passing through scenes or visiting places which they have thought of and dreamed of at home with beating hearts for many years. And yet now that the time has come, and the enjoyment is before them, there is some internal source of disquiet, some mental vexation or annoyance, some secret resentment or heart-burning, arising out of the circumstances in which they are placed, or the relations which they sustain to one another, which destroys their peace and quiet of mind, and of course incapacitates them for any real happiness. So that, on the whole, judging from what I have seen of tourists in Europe, I should say that those that travel do not after all, in general, really pass their time more happily than those who remain at home.

I have two reasons for saying these things. One is, that those of you who have no opportunity to travel, may be more contented to remain at home, and not imagine that those of your friends who go abroad, necessarily pass their time so much more happily than you do. The other reason is, that when you do travel, either in our own country or in foreign lands, you should be more reasonable and considerate, and pay more regard to the wishes and feelings of others, than travellers usually do. Most of the disquietudes and heart-burnings which arise to mar the happiness of parties travelling, come from the selfishness of our hearts, which seems, in some way or other, to bring itself out more into view when we are on a long journey together than at any other time. In the ordinary intercourse of life, this selfishness is covered and concealed by the veil of politeness prescribed by the forms and usages of society. This veil is, however, very thin, and it soon disappears entirely, in the familiar intercourse which is necessarily produced by the incidents and adventures of a journey. In being daily and hourly with each other for a long time, people appear just as they really are; and unless they are really reasonable, considerate, and just towards one another, they are sure sooner or later to disagree.

But though the bridal party were very much out of humor with each other, as we have seen, Mr. George and Rollo were entirely free from any such uneasiness. They both felt very light-hearted and happy. They rambled about the court yard till they had seen all that there was there to interest them, and then they went to their own diligence. They opened the coupe door and looked in.

"Our seats are Nos. 1 and 2," said Rollo.

"Yes," said Mr. George. "One of them is next the window, and the other is in the middle. You may get in first, and take the seat by the window."

"No, uncle George," said Rollo, "you had better have the seat by the window."

"We will take turns for that seat," said Mr. George, "and you shall begin."

Mr. George arranged it to have Rollo take his turn first, because he knew very well that, in the beginning of a journey, such a boy as Rollo was always full of enthusiasm and excitement; and that, consequently, he would enjoy riding at the window much more at first than at a later period. So Rollo got in and took his seat, and Mr. George followed him. In a very few minutes afterwards, the postilions came out with the horses.

But I have something particular to say about the postilions and the horses, and I will say it in the next chapter.

CHAPTER II

THE JOURNEY

There are a great many curious things to be observed in travelling by the public conveyances on the continent of Europe. One is the way of driving the horses. It is a very common thing to have them driven, not by coachmen, but by postilions. There is a postilion for each pair of horses, and he sits upon the nigh horse of the pair. Thus he rides and drives at the same time.

In these cases there is no driver's seat in front of the coach. Or if there is a seat in front, it is occupied by the passengers. All the driving is done by the postilions.

The postilions dress in a sort of livery, which is quite gay in its appearance, being trimmed with red. The collars and the lapels of their jackets, too, are ornamented here and there with figures of stage horns and other emblems of their profession. They also wear enormously long and stout boots. These boots come up above their knees. They carry only a short whip, for they only have to whip the horse that they are upon, and the one which is by the side of him, and so they do not have to reach very far. When there are four horses, there are two postilions, and when there are six, three.

Jacob Abbott

A large diligence, with six horses, and a gayly dressed postilion mounted on one of the horses of each pair, makes a very grand appearance, you may depend, in coming, upon the gallop, into the streets of a town—the postilions cracking their whips, and making as much noise as they can, and all the boys and girls of the street coming to the doors and windows to see.

"I am glad we are going to have postilions, uncle George," said Rollo, as they were getting into the coach.

"Why?" asked Mr. George.

"Because I like the looks of them," said Rollo; "and then we always go faster, too, when we have postilions. Besides, when there is a seat for a driver on the coach, it blocks up our front windows; but now our windows are all clear."

"Those are excellent reasons—all of them," said Mr. George.

The postilions did indeed drive very fast, when they once got upon the road. There was a delay of half an hour, at the gate of the city, for the examination of the passports; during which time the postilions, having dismounted from their horses, stood talking together, and playing off jokes upon each other. At length, when the passports were ready, they sprang into their saddles, and set the horses off upon the run.

The road, on leaving the gates, entered a wide and beauty-ful avenue, which was at this time filled with peasants coming into town, for that day was market day in Naples. The people coming in were dressed in the most curious costumes. Multitudes were on foot, others rode crowded together in donkey carts. Some rode on the backs of donkeys, with a load of farming produce before or behind them. The women, in such cases, sat square upon the donkey's back, with both their feet hanging down on one side; and they banged the donkey with their heels to make him get out of the way so that the diligence could go by.

The country was very rich and beautiful, and it was cultivated every where like a garden. Here and there were groves of mulberries,—the tree on which the silk worm feeds,—and there were vineyards, with the vines just bursting into leaf, and now and then a little garden of orange trees. In the mean time the postilions kept cracking their whips, and the horses galloped on at such a speed that Rollo had scarcely time to see the objects by the road side, they glided so swiftly by.

"Won't the silk worms eat any kind of leaves but mulberry leaves?" he asked.

"No," said Mr. George, "at least the mulberry silk worms will not. There are a great many different kinds of silk worms in the world; that is, there are a great many different kinds of caterpillars that spin a thread and make a ball to wrap up their eggs in, and each one lives on a different plant or tree. If you watch the caterpillars in a garden, you will see that each kind lives on some particular leaf, and will not touch any other."

"Yes," said Rollo, "we found a big caterpillar once on the caraway in our garden, and we shut him up in a box, in order to see what sort of a butterfly he would turn into, and we gave him different kinds of leaves to eat, but he would not eat any but caraway leaves."

"And what became of him at last?" asked Mr. George.

"O, he turned into a butterfly," said Rollo. "First he turned into a chrysalis, and then he turned into a butterfly."

"There are a great many different kinds of silk worms," said Mr. George; "but in order to find one that can be made useful, there are several conditions to be fulfilled."

"What do you mean by conditions to be fulfilled?" asked Rollo.

"Why, I mean that there are several things necessary, in order that the silk worm should be a good one to make silk from. In the first place, the fibre of the silk that he spins must be fine, and also strong. In the next place, it must easily unwind from the cocoon. Then the animal must be a tolerably hardy one, so as to be easily raised in great numbers. Then the plant or tree that it feeds upon must be a thrifty and hardy one, and easily cultivated. The mulberry silk worm has been found to answer to these conditions better than any hitherto known; but there are some others that I believe they are now trying, in order to see if they will not be better still. They are looking about in all parts of the world to see what they can find."

"Who are looking?" asked Rollo.

"The Society of Acclimatation," replied Mr. George. "That is a society founded in Paris, and extending to all parts of the world, that is employed in finding new plants and new animals that can be made useful to man, or finding some that are useful to man in one country, and so introducing them into other countries. They are trying specially to find new silk worms."

"There are some kinds of caterpillars in America," said Rollo, "that wind their silk up into balls. I mean to get some of the balls when I go home, and see if I can unwind them."

"That will be an excellent plan," said Mr. George.

"If I can only find the end," said Rollo.

"There must be some art required to find the end," rejoined Mr. George, "and then I believe there is some preparation which is necessary to make the cocoons unwind."

"I wish I knew what it was," said Rollo.

"You can inquire of some of the people when we stop to dine," replied Mr. George.

"But I don't know enough Italian for that," said Rollo.

"That's a pity," said Mr. George.

In the mean time the horses trotted and galloped on until they had gone about ten miles, and then at length the postilions brought them up at the door of an inn, in a village. Fresh horses were standing all ready at the door, with new postilions. The postilions that had been driving took out their horses and led them away, and then came themselves to the window of the coupe and held out their caps for their *buono mano*, as they call it; that is, for a small present.

Every body in Italy, who performs any service, expects, in addition to being paid the price regularly agreed upon for the service, to receive a present, greater or smaller according to the nature of the case. This present is called the *buono mano*.[2]

Jacob Abbott

[Footnote 2: Pronounced *bono mahno.*]

The postilions always expect a buono mano from the passengers in the stage coach, especially from those who ride in the coupe.

Rollo gave them a few coppers each, for himself and for Mr. George, and just as he had done so, a young man without any hat upon his head, but with a white napkin under his arm, came out of the hotel, and advancing to the window of the coupe asked Mr. George and Rollo, in French, if they wished to take any thing.

"No," said Mr. George. "Not any thing."

"Yes, uncle George," said Rollo, "let us go and see what they have got."

He said this, of course, in English, but immediately changing his language into French, he asked the waiter what they could have.

The waiter said that they could have some hot coffee. There would not be time for any thing else.

"Let us have some hot coffee, uncle George," said Rollo, eagerly.

"Very well,' said Mr. George.

So Rollo gave the order, and the waiter went into the house. In a moment he returned with two cups of very nice coffee, which he brought on a tray. By this time, however, the fresh horses were almost harnessed, so that it was necessary to drink the coffee quick. But there was no difficulty in doing this, for it was very nice, and not too hot. Rollo had barely time to give back the cups and pay for the coffee before the diligence began to move. The postilions started the horses with a strange sort of a cry, that they uttered while standing beside them, and then leaped into the saddles just as they were beginning to run.

The journey was continued much in this way during the whole day. The country was delightful; the road was hard and smooth as a floor, and the horses went very fast. In a word, Rollo had a capital ride.

After traversing a comparatively level country for some miles, the road entered a mountainous region, where there was a long ascent. At the foot of this ascent was a post house, and here they put on six horses instead of four. Of course there were now three postilions. But although the country was mountainous, the ascent was not steep, for the road was carried up by means of long windings and zigzags, in such a manner that the rise was very regular and gradual all the way. The consequence was, that the six horses took the diligence on almost as fast up the mountains as the four had done on the level ground.

About five o'clock in the afternoon the diligence made a good stop, in order to allow the passengers to dine.

"We will go in and take dinner with the rest," said Mr. George, "and so save the things that we have put up for a moonlight supper on the Pontine Marshes."

"Yes," said Rollo, "I shall like that very much. Besides, I want to go and take dinner with them here, for I want to see how they do it."

The place where the diligence stopped was a town called Mola di Gaeta. It stood in a very picturesque situation, near the sea. For though the road, in leaving Naples, had led at first into the interior of the country, and had since been winding about among the mountains, it had now come down again to the margin of the sea.

The entrance to the hotel was under a great archway. There were doors to the right and left from this archway, leading to staircases and to apartments. The passengers from the diligence were conducted through one of these doors into a very ancient looking hall, where there was a table set for dinner, with plates enough for twenty persons—that being about the number of passengers contained in the various compartments of the diligence.

On the opposite side of the arched way was a door leading to another hall, where there was a table set for the conductor and the postilions.

After waiting a few minutes, the company of passengers took their seats at the table. Besides the plates for the guests, there was a row of dishes extending up and down the middle of the table, containing apples, pears, oranges, nuts, raisins, little cakes, and bon-bons of various kinds. There were also in this row two vases containing flowers.

Excepting these fruits and sweetmeats, there was nothing eatable upon the table when the guests sat down. It is not customary in European dinners to put any thing upon the table except the dessert.

The other dishes are brought round, and presented one by one to each guest. First came the soup. When the soup had been eaten, and the soup plates had been removed, then there was boiled beef. The beef was upon two dishes, one for each side of the table. It was cut very nicely in slices, and each dish had a fork and a spoon in it, for the guests to help themselves with. The dishes were carried along the sides of the table by the waiters, and offered to each guest, the guests helping themselves in succession to such pieces as they liked.

After the beef had been eaten, the plates were all changed, and then came a course of fried potatoes; then, after another change of plates, a course of mutton chops; then green peas; then roast beef; then cauliflower with drawn butter; then roast chicken with salad; and lastly, some puddings. For each separate article of all this dinner there was a fresh plate furnished to each guest.

After the pudding plates were removed, small plates for the dessert were furnished; and then the fruit, and the nuts, and the bon-bons were served; and the dinner was over.

For every two guests there was a decanter of wine. At least it was what they called wine, though in taste it was more like sour cider. The people generally used it by pouring a little of it into their water.

When the dinner was over, the passengers all paid the amount that was charged for it, and each gave, besides, a buono mano to the waiter who had waited upon his side of the table. By this time the diligence was ready, and they all went and took their seats in it again.

The sun was now going down, and in the course of an hour the last of its rays were seen gilding the summits of the mountains. Soon afterwards the evening began to come on.

"Before a great while," said Mr. George, "we shall begin to draw near to the frontier."

"Yes," said Rollo, "the frontier between the kingdom of Naples and the dominions of the pope. They will examine the baggage there, I suppose."

"No," said Mr. George; "they will not examine the baggage till we get to Rome."

"I thought they always examined the baggage at the frontier, when we came into any new country," said Rollo.

"They do," said Mr. George, "unless the baggage is under the charge of public functionaries; and then, to save time, they often take it into the capital, and examine it there. I asked one of the passengers at the dinner table, and he said that the trunks were not to be opened till we get to Rome."

"They will examine the passports, I suppose," said Rollo.

"Yes," replied Mr. George, "they will, undoubtedly, examine the passports at the frontier."

You cannot pass from one country in Europe to another, any where, without stopping at the last military station of the country that you leave, to have your passport examined and stamped, in token of permission given you to go out, and also at the first military station of the country which you are about to enter, to have them examined and stamped again, in token of permission to come in. All this, as you may suppose, is very troublesome. Besides that, there are fees to pay, which, in the course of a long journey, amount to a considerable sum.

Besides the passport business which was to be attended to, there was a grand change of the diligence establishment at the frontier. The coach itself, which came from Naples, and also the conductor and postilions, were all left at the border, and the passengers were transferred to a new turnout which came from Rome. Indeed, there was a double change; for the Roman diligence brought a load of passengers from Rome to meet the Neapolitan one at the border, and thus each company of travellers had to be transferred to the establishment belonging to the country which they were entering.

This change was made in a post house, in a solitary place near the frontier. It caused a detention of nearly an hour, there were so many formalities to go through. It was late in the evening, and the work was done by the light of torches and lanterns. The two diligences were backed up against each other, and then all the trunks and baggage were transferred from the top of one coach to the top of the other, without being taken down at all. The baggage in these diligences is always packed upon the top.

You would think that this would make the coach top heavy, and so it does in some degree; but then the body of the coach below is so large and heavy, that the extra weight above is well counterpoised; and then, besides, the roads are so smooth and level, and withal so hard, that there is no danger of an upset.

The work of shifting the baggage from one diligence to the other was performed under an archway. There was a door leading from this archway into a large office, where the two companies of passengers were assembled, waiting for the coaches to be ready. All these passengers were loaded with carpet bags, knapsacks, valises, bundles of umbrellas and canes, and other such light baggage which they had had with them inside the coaches. Many of them were sitting on chairs and benches around the sides of the room, with their baggage near them. Others were walking about the room, changing money with each other; that is, those that were going from Rome to Naples were changing the Roman money, which they had left, for Neapolitan money. The money of one of these countries does not circulate well in the other country. In the middle of the room was a great table, where the conductors and other officials were at work with papers and accounts. Rollo could not understand what they were doing.

Rollo walked about the office, looking at the different passengers, and observing what was going on, while Mr. George remained near the coaches, to watch the transfer of the baggage.

"I want to be sure," said Mr. George, "that our trunk is there, and that they shift it over to the Roman coach."

"They are changing money inside," said Rollo. "Have you got any that you want to have changed?"

"No," said Mr. George. "I did not know that we could change here; and I calculated closely, and planned it so as not to have any of the Naples money left."

"I have got only two or three pieces," said Rollo, "and those I am going to carry home to America for coins."

At length the changes were completed, and Mr. George and Rollo, and also all the other passengers who had come in the diligence from Naples, began to take their places in the coach for Rome; while at the same time the other company got into the Naples coach, which was now going to return. The conductor came for his *buono mano*, the new horses were harnessed in, the postilions leaped into the saddles, and thus both parties set out upon their night ride. It was not far from nine o'clock.

"And now," said Mr. George, "before a great while we shall come upon the Pontine Marshes."

The Pontine Marshes form an immense tract of low and level land, which have been known and celebrated in history for nearly two thousand years. Though called marshes, they are so far drained by ancient canals that the land is firm enough for grass to grow upon it, and for flocks of sheep and herds of cattle to feed; but yet it is so low and so unhealthy, that it is utterly uninhabitable by man. The extent of these marshes is immense. The road traverses them in a direct line, and on a perfect level, for twenty-five or thirty miles, without passing a single habitation, except the post houses, and in the middle a solitary inn.

And yet there is nothing desolate or dreary in the aspect of the Pontine Marshes. On the contrary the view on every side, in passing across them, is extremely beautiful. The road is wide, and smooth, and level, and is bordered on each side with a double row of very ancient and venerable trees, which give to it, for the whole distance, the character of a magnificent avenue. Think of a broad and handsome avenue, running straight as an arrow for twenty-five miles!

Beyond the trees, on one side, there is a wide canal. This canal runs parallel to the road, and you often meet boats coming or going upon it. Beyond the canal, and beyond the trees on the other side, there extends, as far as the eye can reach, one vast expanse of living green, as smooth and beautiful as can be imagined. This immense tract of meadow is divided here and there by hedges or palings, and now and then a pretty grove appears to vary the scene. Immense flocks of sheep, and herds of horses and cattle, are seen feeding every where, and sometimes herdsmen, on horseback galloping to and fro, attending to their charge.

Mr. George and Rollo had had a fine opportunity to see the scenery of the Pontine Marshes when they came to Naples, for then they crossed them by day light. Now, however, it was night, and there was not much to be seen except the gnarled and venerable trunks of the trees, on each side of the road, as the light of the diligence lanterns flashed upon them.

The postilions drove exceedingly fast all the way over the marshes. The stage stopped three times to change horses. Mr. George kept up a continual conversation with Rollo all the way, in order to prevent him from going to sleep; for, as I have said before, it is considered dangerous to sleep while on the marshes.

About midnight Rollo proposed that they should eat their supper.

"No," said Mr. George, "we will keep our supper for the last thing. As long as we can keep awake without it we will."

So they went on for two hours longer. About one o'clock the moon rose, and the moonbeams shining in through the windows of the coupe, enlivened the interior very much.

"The moonlight makes it a great deal pleasanter," said Rollo.

"Yes," said Mr. George, "and it will make it a great deal more convenient for us to eat our supper."

The diligence stopped at a post house to change horses, a little before two, and immediately after it set out again. Mr. George said that it was time for them to take their supper. So Rollo opened the two bags, and took out from one the chicken and the two rolls, and from the other the bottle of coffee and the oranges. He placed the things, as he took them out, in a large pocket before him, in the front of the coupe. Mr. George took two newspapers out of his knapsack, one for Rollo and one for himself, to spread in their laps while they were eating. Then, with a sharp blade of his pocket knife, he began to carve the chicken.

The chicken was very tender, and the rolls were very nice; and as, moreover, both the travellers were quite hungry, they found the supper in all respects excellent. For drink, they had the juice of the oranges. To drink this juice, they cut a round hole in one end of the orange, and then run the blade of the knife in, in all directions, so as to break up the pulp. They could then drink out the juice very conveniently.

At the close of the supper they drank the coffee. The coffee was cold, it is true, but it was very good, and it made an excellent ending to the meal.

They made the supper last as long as possible, in order to occupy the time. It was three o'clock before it was finished and the papers cleared away. At half past three, Rollo, in looking out at the window, saw a sort of bank by the side of the road; and on observing attentively, he perceived that there was a curve in the road itself, before them.

"Uncle George," said he, "we have got off the marshes!"

"I verily believe we have," said Mr. George.

"So now we may go to sleep," said Rollo.

"Yes," said Mr. George. "I'll lay my head over into the corner, and you may lie against my shoulder."

So Mr. George and Rollo placed themselves in as comfortable a position as possible, and composed themselves to sleep. They slept several hours; waking up, or, rather, half waking up, once during the interval, while the diligence stopped for the purpose of changing horses. When they finally awoke, the sun was up high, and was shining in quite bright through the coupe windows.

CHAPTER III

THE ARRIVAL AT ROME

When Mr. George and Rollo awoke from their sleep, they found that they were coming into the environs of Rome. The country was green and beautiful, but it seemed almost uninhabited; and in every direction were to be seen immense ruins of tombs, and aqueducts, and other such structures, now gone to decay. There was an ancient road leading out of Rome in this direction, called the *Appian Way*. It was by this road that the apostle Paul travelled, in making his celebrated journey to Rome, after appealing from the Jewish jurisdiction to that of Caesar. Indeed, the Appii Forum and the Three Taverns, places mentioned in the account of this journey contained in the Acts, were on the very road that Mr. George and Rollo had been travelling in their journey from Naples to Rome.

The remains of the Appian Way are still to be traced for many miles south of Rome. The road was paved, in ancient times, with very large blocks of an exceedingly hard kind of stone. These stones were of various shapes, but they were fitted together and flattened on the top, and thus they made a very smooth, and at the same time a very solid, pavement. In many places along the Appian Way this old pavement still remains, and is as good as ever.

Jacob Abbott

At length the diligence arrived at the gate of the city. It passed through an arched gateway, leading through an ancient and very venerable wall, and then stopped at the door of a sort of office just within. There were two soldiers walking to and fro before the office.

"What are we stopping for here?" asked Rollo.

"For the passports, I suppose," said Mr. George.

The conductor of the diligence came to the door of the coupe and asked for the passports. Mr. George gave him his and Rollo's, and the conductor carried them, together with those which he had obtained from the other passengers, into the office. He then ordered the postilions to drive on.

"How shall we get our passports again?" asked Rollo.

"We must send for them to the police office, I suppose," said Mr. George.

It is very customary, in the great capitals of Europe, for the police to take the passports of travellers, on their arrival at the gates of the city, and direct them to send for them at the central police office on the following day.

After passing the gate, the diligence went on a long way, through a great many narrow streets, leading into the heart of the city. There was nothing in these streets to denote the ancient grandeur of Rome, excepting now and then an old and venerable ruin, standing neglected among the other buildings.

Rollo, however, in looking out at the windows of the coupe, saw a great many curious sights, as the diligence drove along. Among these one of the most remarkable was a procession of people dressed in a most fantastic manner, and wearing masks which entirely concealed their faces. There were two round holes in the masks for the eyes. Mr. George told Rollo that these were men doing penance. They had been condemned to walk through the streets in this way, as a punishment for some of their sins.

"Why, they treat them just as if they were children," said Rollo.

"They *are* children," said Mr. George, "in every thing but years."

Not long after this, Rollo saw a very magnificent carriage coming along. It was perfectly resplendent with crimson and gold. The horses, too, and the coachman, and the footmen, were gorgeously caparisoned and apparelled in the same manner.

Rollo pointed it out to Mr. George. Mr. George said it was a cardinal's carriage.

"I wish the cardinal was in it," said Rollo. "I would like to have seen him."

"I presume he would have looked very much like any other man," replied Mr. George.

"Yes, but he would have been dressed differently, wouldn't he?"

"Perhaps so," said Mr. George.

"Perhaps he would have had his red hat on," said Rollo. "I

Jacob Abbott

should like to see a cardinal wearing his red hat."

The badge of the cardinal's office is a hat and dress of a red color.

At length the diligence passed under an archway which led into a large open court, similar to the one in Naples where the journey had been commenced. The passengers got out, the horses were unharnessed, and the baggage was taken down. The trunks were all taken into an office pertaining to the custom house, to be examined by the officers there, in order to see whether there were any contraband goods in them.

Mr. George unlocked his trunk and lifted up the lid. An officer came up to the place, and patting with his hand upon the top of the clothes, as if to prevent Mr. George from lifting them up to show what was below, he said,—

"Very well; very well; it is sufficient."

So saying, he shut down the top of the trunk again, and marked it, "Passed." He then touched his hat, and asked Mr. George if he would make some small present for the benefit of the custom house officers.

That is to say, he evaded the performance of his duty as an officer of the customs, in expectation that the traveller would pay him for his delinquency. Most travellers are very willing to pay in such cases. They have various articles in their trunks which they have bought in other countries, and which, strictly speaking, are subject to duty in entering Rome, and they are willing to pay a fee rather than to have their trunks overhauled. Others, of more sturdy morality, refuse to pay these fees. They consider them as of the nature of bribes. So they say to the officers,—

"Examine the baggage as much as you please, and if you find any duties due, I will pay them. But I will not pay any bribes."

"Now, Rollo," said Mr. George, when he had got possession of his trunk, "we want a carriage to take us and the baggage to the hotel. You may go and see if you can find one, and I will stay here and look after the baggage. Engage the carriage by the hour."

So Rollo went out of the court, and soon found a carriage. Before he got into it, he said to the coachman,—

"*Per hora!*"

This means, By the hour.

At the same time Rollo held up his watch to the coach-man, in order to let him see what o'clock it was.

"*Si, signore*," said the coachman.

Si, signore, is the Italian for Yes, sir.

Rollo could not say in Italian where he wished the coachman to go, and so he stood up in the carriage and pointed. Following his indications, the coachman drove in through the archway to the court of the post office, where he found Mr. George waiting. The trunk and the bags were put upon the carriage, in front, and Mr. George got in with Rollo.

"Hotel d'Amerique," said Mr. George to the coachman.

"*Si, signore*," said the coachman, and immediately he began to drive away.

The Hotel d'Amerique was the one where Mr. George had concluded to go. He had found the name and a description of this hotel in his guide book.

"Why did you want me to take the carriage by the hour?" asked Rollo.

"Because it is very probable," said Mr. George, "that we shall not get in at the Hotel d'Amerique, and in that case we shall have to go to other hotels, and unless we take him by the hour, he would charge a course for every hotel that we go to, and the charge even for *two* courses, is more than for an hour."

The event showed that Mr. George was right in his calculations. The Hotel d'Amerique was full. The waiter, who came out, as soon as he saw the carriage stop at the door, told Mr. George this in French.

"Then please tell our coachman," said Mr. George, "to drive us to any other principal hotel that is near here, and if that is full, to another; and so on, until he finds a good place where they can take us in."

Mr. George said this, of course, in French. The waiter delivered the message to the coachman in Italian.

"Yes," said the coachman, to himself, "that I'll do. But I shall take good care that you don't find any place where you can get in this two hours, if I can help it."

The reason why the coachman did not wish that his travellers should find a hotel soon was, of course, because he wished to earn as much money as possible by driving them about.

He immediately began to think what hotels would be most likely to be full, and drove first to those. The first of all was a hotel, situated quite near one of the gates of the city, the one where the principal entrance is for all travellers coming from the north. It is called the "Gate of the People,"—or in Italian, *Porto del Popolo*. The gate opens into a large triangular space, which is called the *Piazza del Popolo. Piazza*,[3] in Italian, means a public square.

[Footnote 3: Pronounced *Piatza*.]

This Piazza del Popolo is one of the most celebrated places in Rome. There are three streets that radiate from it directly through the heart of the town. Between the centre and the two side streets, at the corners where they come out upon the square, are two churches exactly alike. They are called sometimes the *twin churches*, on this account.

The Piazza del Popolo is a great place for public parades. On one side is a high ascent, with a broad expanse of gardens upon the top, and zigzag roads, handsomely walled up, and ornamented with statues and fountains, and with marble seats placed here and there for foot passengers to rest themselves upon, when ascending.

Every year, at the end of what they call Holy Week, they have a great celebration of fireworks from the side of this hill and from the terrace above; and then all the people assemble in the Piazza below to witness them.

But I must go back to Mr. George and Rollo. The coachman stopped at a large hotel, fronting upon this square. On inquiring at the bureau, (on the continent of Europe they call an office a bureau) Mr. George found that all the rooms were occupied except one large apartment, of four rooms. This was, of course, more than Mr. George wanted.

At the next hotel where the coachman stopped, there were no rooms at all vacant, and at the next only one small room, with a single narrow bed in it.

"If we can't find any other," said Rollo, "we will come back and take this, and I will sleep on the floor."

"O, no!" said Mr. George.

"Why, uncle George!" said Rollo, "I can make it very comfortable on the floor, by rolling up two coats or cloaks into two long rolls, and wedging them in under me, one on one side of me and the other on the other, and then putting a carpet bag under my head for a pillow. It feels just as if you were in a good bed."

Mr. George smiled, and got into the carriage again, and the coachman drove on.

After a while, he stopped at the door of a hotel which stood in rather a retired place among narrow streets, though there was an open space in front of it. Mr. George inquired for rooms here, and the waiter said that they had one left.

"Are there two beds in it?" asked Mr. George.

"No, sir," said the waiter, "but we can put two beds in. Would you like to go and see it, sir?"

"No," said Mr. George, "I will take it without going to see it. It is the best that we can do."

So the porter of the hotel took off the baggage, while Mr. George paid the coachman for an hour and a half of time. Mr. George and Rollo then followed the porter to their room. In order to reach it, they had to ascend several stories, up massive staircases of stone, and then to go out to the extreme end of a long corridor. The room, when they came to it, proved to be quite small, and there was but one bed in it. There was, however, room for another; and the waiter, who had followed them up, said that he would cause another one to be put in without any delay.

CHAPTER IV

A RAMBLE

"And now, uncle George," said Rollo, "we'll get ready, and then the first thing that we will do, will be to go down into the dining room and get some breakfast."

"Why, we have had our breakfast already," said Mr. George. "We had it at two o'clock this morning, on the Pontine Marshes."

"O, no," said Rollo, "that was our supper for last night."

"Very well," said Mr. George, "we will have some breakfast. You may go down and order it as soon as you are ready. I will come down by the time that it is on the table."

"What shall I order?" asked Rollo.

"Whatever you please," said Mr. George.

Accordingly Rollo, as soon as he was ready, went down stairs, and looking about in the entrance hall, he saw a door with the words TABLE D'HOTE, in gilt letters, over it.

"Ah," said he to himself, "this is the place."

He opened the door, and found himself in a long, narrow room, which seemed, however, more like a passage way than like a room. There was a sort of rack on one side of it for hats and coats. There were several pictures in this room, with prices marked upon them, as if they were for sale, and also a number of very pretty specimens of marble, and inlaid paper weights, and models of columns, temples, and ruins of various kinds, and other such curiosities as are kept every where in Rome to sell to visitors. Rollo looked at all these things as he passed through the room, considering, as he examined them, whether his uncle George would probably wish to buy any of them.

One of them was a model of a column, with a spiral line of sculptures extending from the base to the summit. These sculptures represented figures of men and horses, sometimes in battle, sometimes crossing bridges, and sometimes in grand processions entering a town.

"This must be a model of some old column in Rome, I suppose," said Rollo to himself. "Perhaps I shall find it some time or other, when I am rambling about the streets. But now I must go and see about breakfast."

So saying, Rollo passed on to the end of the passage way, where there was a door with curtains hanging before it. He pushed these curtains aside, opened the door, and went in. He found himself ushered into a dining room, with a long table extending up and down the centre of it. There was a row of massive columns on each side of the table, which supported the vaultings of the ceiling above. In different parts of this table there were small parties of gentlemen and ladies, engaged in taking late breakfasts.

Jacob Abbott

Rollo walked down on one side of the table. There was on that side a party consisting of a lady and gentleman with two children, a girl and a boy,—all dressed in such a manner as to give them a foreign air. The gentleman was speaking to the waiter in French when Rollo passed by the party. The boy was sitting next to one of the great pillars. These pillars were so near the table that each one of them took the place of a seat.

Rollo walked on and took his seat next beyond the pillar. Of course the pillar was between him and the boy.

In a few minutes a waiter came to ask what Rollo would have for breakfast. He asked in French. Rollo gave an order for breakfast for two. He said that his uncle would be down in a few minutes.

"Very well, sir," said the waiter.

As soon as the waiter had gone, Rollo looked round the other way, and he saw that the other boy was peeping at him from behind the pillar. The boy laughed when he caught Rollo's eye, and Rollo laughed too. The boy seemed to be about nine years old.

A moment afterwards the boy began to peep at Rollo from behind the pillar on the back side, and then again on the front side, thus playing a sort of bo-peep. In this way, in a few minutes the two boys began to feel quite acquainted with each other, without, however, having spoken a word. They would, perhaps, have continued this game longer, but just at this moment the breakfast for the party came in, and the boy set himself at work eating a warm roll, buttered, and drinking his coffee.

"Can you speak French?" asked Rollo,—of course

speaking French himself in asking the question.

"Yes," said the boy, "but not very well."

"Then," said Rollo to himself, "he cannot be a French boy. Perhaps he is an Italian boy."

"Italian?" asked Rollo.

"No," said the boy, "not at all. All I know of Italian is *grazia*."[4]

[Footnote 4: Pronounced *gratzia*.]

"What does that mean?" asked Rollo.

"It means, Thank you," said the boy.

"He must be a German boy, I think," said Rollo to himself.

After pausing a moment, Rollo ventured to ask the boy what his name was.

"Charles Beekman," said the boy. He pronounced the name in so English a fashion, that Rollo perceived at once that he must speak English, so he changed from French to English himself, and said,—

"So you are an English boy."

"No," said Charles, "I'm an American boy."

Rollo here laughed outright, to think how much trouble they had both been taking to speak to each other in French, each supposing the other to be some outlandish foreigner, when, after all, they were both Americans, and could talk perfectly well together in their own mother tongue. Such adventures as these, however, are very frequently met with, in travelling in foreign countries.

After finding that they could both speak English, the two boys talked with each other like old friends, for some minutes; and at length finding that the pillar between them was very much in the way, Charles, with his mother's permission, moved his seat round to Rollo's side of it, Rollo himself moving to the next chair, to make room for him. Mrs. Beekman readily consented to this, having first observed that Rollo appeared to be a boy of agreeable and gentlemanly manners and demeanor.

When Mr. George at length came down, he was at first quite surprised to find that Rollo had thus obtained a companion; but before the breakfast was completed, he had become quite well acquainted with the Beekman family himself. Towards the end of the breakfast Rollo said that he was going out to take a walk, and he asked Mrs. Beekman to let Charles go with him. Mr. George was going to finish some letters in his room, and was then going to the post office and to the bankers, where Rollo did not particularly wish to go.

"It will be better for you and me to go out and take a walk by ourselves," said he to Charles, "if your mother is willing."

"Yes," said Mrs. Beekman, "I am willing. Only you must take care and not get lost."

"O, no," said Rollo; "I'll take care of that. Besides, if we should get lost, I know exactly what to do."

"What would you do?" asked Mr. Beekman.

"I would just take a carriage," replied Rollo, "and order the coachman to drive right to the hotel."

"Very good," said Mr. Beekman, "that would do very well."

Accordingly, after breakfast Mr. George went to his room to finish his letters, while Rollo and Charlie set out on their walk, to see what they could see of Rome.

Rollo's plan of taking a carriage, in case of getting lost in a strange city, and ordering the coachman to drive to the hotel, is a very excellent one; but one thing is quite essential to the success of it, and that is, that the person lost should know the name of his hotel. Unfortunately, Rollo was going out without this requisite. Neither he himself nor Mr. George had observed the name of the hotel where the coachman whom they had employed, on their arrival, had finally left them; and in going out Rollo forgot to observe what it was. He did not even take notice of the name of the street. He did observe, however, that the hotel had a small open space, like a square, before it, with a fountain on one side. The water from the fountain flowed into a small stone basin, with curious figures sculptured on the side of it.

"Let us go and look at this basin," said Charles, "and see if it would not be a good place for us to sail little boats."

The basin was in a cool and pleasant place, being overshadowed by the drooping branches of a great tree. Rollo, however, did not wish to stay by it long.

"Let us go now and see the streets of Rome," said he; "we

can come out and look at this basin at any time."

So the two boys walked along, paying little attention to the direction in which they were going.

"We shall find some of the great streets pretty soon," said Rollo, "and then we will take an observation."

"What do you mean by that?" asked Charles.

"Why, we will take particular notice of some great building, or something else that is remarkable where we come out into the street, and by that means we shall be able to find our way back to the hotel."

"Yes," said Charles, "that will be an excellent plan."

So the boys went on, and presently they came out into what seemed to be quite a busy street. It was not very wide, but it was bordered with gay-looking shops on each side. These shops were for the sale of models, specimens of marbles, Etruscan vases, mosaics, cameos, and other such things which are sold to visitors in Rome. The number of mosaics and cameos was very great. They were displayed in little show cases, placed outside the shops, under the windows and before the doors, so that people could examine them as they walked along.

"O, what a quantity of mosaics and *cameos*!" exclaimed Rollo.

"What are mosaics and cameos?" asked Charles.

As perhaps some of the readers of this book may not know precisely the meaning of these words, I will here explain to them, as Rollo did to Charles, how mosaics and cameos are made.

In the first place, in respect to cameos. Imagine a small flat piece of stone, of different colors on the two sides, say white and black. We will suppose that the white extends half through the thickness of the stone, and that the remaining part of the thickness is black. Stones are often found with such a division of colors, not only white and black, but of all other hues.

Now, the artist takes such a stone as this, and marks out some design upon one side of it, say upon the white side. Perhaps the design may be the figure of a man. Then he cuts away all the white of the stone except the figure; and the result is, that he has the figure of the man, or whatever else his design may be, in white, on a black ground, and the whole in one piece of stone, all solid.

Besides stone, shell is often used for cameos; many shells being pink, or of some other such color on the inside, and white towards the outside. In such a case, the figures of the design would be pink, or whatever else the color of the stone might be, on a white ground.

The artists of Rome are celebrated for making beautiful cameos, both in shell and in stone. The figures are very nicely drawn, and are very beautifully cut, and when finished are set as pins, bracelets, and other ornaments.

The *mosaics*, on the other hand, are made in a very different way. In these, the design is represented by different colored stones or bits of glass worked in together, with great care, in an opening made in the material serving for the groundwork. Rollo and Charlie went into one of the shops, and saw a man making one of these mosaics. He was working at a table. On one side was a small painting on a card, which was his model. He was copying this painting in mosaic. The bits of glass that he was working with were in the form of slender bars, not much larger than a stiff bristle. They were of all imaginable colors—the several colors being each kept by itself, in the divisions of a box on the table. The man took up these bars, one by one, and broke off small pieces of them, of the colors that he wanted, with a pair of pincers, and set them into the work. He put them in perpendicularly, and the lower ends went into some soft composition, placed there to receive and hold them. The upper ends, of course, came together at the surface of the work.

The man who was making the mosaic told Rollo, that as soon as he had finished placing the pieces for the whole design, he should grind off the surface so as to make it smooth, and polish it. It would then have the appearance of a painted picture.

You would think that as the colors of the design are thus represented by separate pieces of glass, put in one after the other, the result would be a sort of mottled appearance, or at least that the gradations of hue would be sharp and harsh in their effect. But it is not so. The pieces are so small, and the different shades succeed each other so regularly, that when viewed from the ordinary distance, the junctions disappear altogether, and the shades mingle and blend together in the softest and most perfect manner.

The mosaic which the workman was making in the shop where Rollo and Charles went in, was a small one, intended to form part of a bracelet. There were, however, some in the same shop that were quite large. They were framed like pictures, and were hanging up against the wall. Indeed, there was nothing but the circumstance that they were in a mosaic shop, to denote that they were not pictures, beautifully painted in oil. One was a landscape; another was a portrait of a beautiful girl; another was a basket of fruit and flowers.

In some of the churches of Rome, there are mosaics of very large size, which are exact and beautiful copies of some of the most celebrated paintings in the world. Strangers coming into the churches and looking at these pictures, never imagine them to be mosaics, and when they are told that they are so, they can scarcely believe the story. But on examining them very near, or in looking at them through an opera glass,—for sometimes you cannot get very near them,—you can easily see the demarcations between the little stones.

It is a very curious circumstance that the most ancient pictures in the churches of Rome and Italy are mosaics, and not paintings. Mosaics seem to have come first in the history of art, and paintings followed, in imitation of them. Indeed, the arranging of different colored stones in a pavement, or in a floor, so as to represent some ornamental design, would naturally be the first attempt at decoration made in the construction of buildings. Then would follow casing the walls with different colored marbles, arranged in pretty ways, and finally the representation of men and animals would be attempted. This we find, from an examination of ancient monuments, was the actual course of things, and painting in oil came in at the end as an imitation of pictures in stone.

Rollo and Charles were induced to go into the mosaic shop by the invitation of the workman, whose table, as it happened, stood near the door. He saw the two boys looking in somewhat wistfully, as they went by, and he invited them to walk in. He saw at once from their appearance that they were visitors that had just arrived in town, and though he did not expect that they would buy any of his mosaics themselves, he thought that there might be ladies in their party who would come and buy, if he treated the boys politely. It was on that account that he invited them to come in. And when they had looked about the establishment as much as they wished, and were ready to go away, he gave them each one of his cards, and asked them to give the cards to the ladies of their party.

"But there are no ladies of my party," said Rollo.

"Who is of your party?" asked the workman.

"Only a young gentleman," said Rollo.

"O, very well," rejoined the man, "that will do just as well. He will certainly wish to buy mosaics, while he is in Rome, for some of the young ladies of his acquaintance."

"I think that is very doubtful," said Rollo; "but nevertheless I will give him the card."

So Rollo and Charles bade the mosaic man good by, and went away.

They had been so much interested in what they had seen in the mosaic shop, and their attention, now that they had left it, was so much occupied with looking at the display of mosaics and cameos which they saw in the little show cases along the street, that Rollo forgot entirely his resolve to take an observation, so as not to lose his way. The boys walked on together until they came to a long and straight, though not very wide street, which was so full of animation and bustle, and was bordered, moreover, on each side by so many gay looking shops, that Rollo said he was satisfied it must be one of the principal streets of the town.

It was, in fact, the principal street in the town. The street is called *the Corso*. It runs in a straight line from the Porto del Popolo, which I have already described, into the very heart of the city. It is near the inner end of this street that the great region of ancient ruins begins.

Rollo and Charles began to walk along the Corso, looking at the shops as they went on. They were obliged, however, to walk in the middle of the street, for the sidewalks, where there were any, were so narrow and irregular as to be of very little service. Indeed, almost all the pedestrians walked in the middle of the street. Now and then a carriage came along, it is true, but the people in that case opened to the right and left, and let it go by.

After going on for some distance, Charles began to look about him somewhat uneasily.

"Rollo," said he, "are you sure that we can find our way home again?"

"O! I forgot about the way home," said Rollo; "but never mind; I can find it easily enough. I can inquire. What is the name of the hotel?"

"I don't know," said Charles.

"Don't know?" repeated Rollo, in a tone of surprise. "Don't know the name of the hotel where you are lodging?"

"No," said Charles, "we only came last night, and I don't know the name of the hotel at all."

"Nor of the street that it is in?" asked Rollo.

"No," said Charles.

"Then," said Rollo, in rather a desponding tone, "I don't know what we shall do."

Just then a carriage was seen coming along; and Rollo and Charles, who had stopped suddenly in the middle of the street, in their surprise and alarm, were obliged to run quick to get out of the way. The carriage was a very elegant one in red and gold, and there were two elegantly dressed footmen standing behind.

"That must be a cardinal's carriage," said Rollo, when the carriage had gone by.

"How do you know?" asked Charles.

"Uncle George told me about them," said Rollo. "You see Rome and all the country about here is under the government of the pope, and the chief officers of his government are the cardinals; and uncle George told me that they ride about in elegant carriages, in red and gold, very splendid and gay. We saw one of them, too, when we were coming into town."

Charles watched the carriage a minute or two, until it had gone some distance away, and then turning to Rollo again, he said,—

"And how about finding our way home again, Rollo?"

"Ah!" said Rollo, "in regard to that I don't know. We shall have to take a carriage when we want to go home, so we may as well go on and have our walk out. We are lost now, and we can't be any more lost go where we will."

So the boys walked on. Presently they came to a large square, with an immense column standing in the centre of it. This column was so similar to the little model which Rollo had seen at the hotel, that he exclaimed at once that it was the same. It had a spiral line of sculptures winding round and round it, from the base to the summit. The figures, however, were very much corroded and worn away, as were indeed all the angles and edges of the base, and of the capital of the column, by the tooth of time. The column had been standing there for eighteen or twenty centuries.

"I saw a model of that very column," said Rollo, "in a little room at the hotel. It is the column of Trajan. I'll prove it to you."

So Rollo asked a gentleman, who was standing on the sidewalk with a Murray's Guide Book in his hand, and who Rollo knew, by that circumstance, was an English or American visitor, if that was not the column of Trajan.

"No," said the gentleman; "it is the column of Antonine."

Rollo looked somewhat abashed at receiving this answer, which turned his attempt to show off his learning to Charles into a ridiculous failure.

"I thought it was called the column of Trajan," said he.

The gentleman, who, as it happened, was an Englishman, made no reply to this observation, but quietly took out an opera glass from a case, which was strapped over his shoulder, and began studying the sculptures on the column.

Jacob Abbott

So Rollo and Charles walked away.

"I believe the name of it is the column of Trajan," said Rollo, "for I saw the name of it on the model at the hotel. That man has just come, and he don't know."

"Are you sure it is the same column?" suggested Charles.

"Yes," said Rollo, "for it was exactly of that shape, and it had the same spiral line of images going round and round it, and a statue on the top. See, how old and venerable it looks! It was built almost two thousand years ago."

"What did they build it for?" asked Charles.

"Why, I don't know exactly," said Rollo, looking a little puzzled; "for ornament, I suppose."

"But I don't see much ornament," said Charles, "in a big column standing all by itself, and with nothing for it to keep up."

"But it *has* something to keep up," rejoined Rollo. "Don't you see, there is a statue on the top of it."

"If that's what it is to keep up," said Charles, "I don't see any sense in making the column so tall as to hold up the statue so high that we can't see it."

"Nor I," said Rollo, "but they often made tall columns, like these, in ancient times."

After rambling about a short time longer, the boys came to another open space, where there was a second column very similar in appearance to the first.

"Ah!" said Rollo, "perhaps this is the column of Trajan."

Rollo was right this time. There are several large columns standing among the ruins of Rome, and among them are two with spiral lines of sculpture around them, which are extremely similar to each other, and it is not at all surprising that Rollo was at first deceived by the resemblance between them.

These columns were built in honor of the victories of great generals, and the spiral lines of sculptures were representations of their different exploits. The statue upon the top of the column was, originally, that of the man in whose honor the column was erected. But in the case of the Roman columns, these original statues have been taken down, and replaced by bronze images of saints, or of the Virgin Mary.

Near the column of Trajan was a large sunken space, in the middle of the square, with a railing around it. In the bottom of this sunken space was a pavement, which looked very old, and rising from it were rows of columns with the tops broken off. The old pavement was eight or ten feet below the level of the street.

"This must be some old ruin or other," said Rollo; "a temple perhaps."

"Only I do not see," said Charles, "why they built their temples down so low."

"Nor do I," said Rollo.

"But, Rollo," said Charles, "I think it is time for us to begin to try to find our way home. I don't see how you are going to find the way at all."

"If I only knew the name of the hotel, or even the name of the street," said Rollo, "I should know at once what to do."

CHAPTER V

GETTING LOST

"And now," said Rollo, "the first thing is to find somebody that can speak French or English, for us to inquire of."

"What good will that do?" asked Charles, "as long as we don't know what to ask them for?"

"True," said Rollo. "That's a real difficulty. I wish we just knew the name of the hotel. At any rate, we will walk along until we find a carriage, and I will be thinking what we had better do."

The boys walked along together. Charles kept silence, so as not to interrupt Rollo in his thinking.

"All I know," said Rollo, after a short pause, "is, that the long, straight street that we came through, is the Corso. I have heard of that street before. If we could only find our way to the Corso, I believe that I could follow it along, and at last find the mosaic shop, and so get back to our hotel."

"Very well," said Charles, "let us try."

Jacob Abbott

"Or, we might get into a carriage," said Rollo, "and direct the coachman which way to drive by pointing."

"So we could," said Charles. "And I should like that, for I am tired of walking so much."

"Then we will get a carriage," said Rollo. "We will take the first one that we see. You shall get inside, and I will mount upon the box with the coachman, and show him which way to go."

"No," said Charles, "we will both get inside, for we can stand up there and point."

"So we can," said Rollo.

There are carriages to be found almost every where in the streets of Rome, especially in the neighborhood of the most interesting ruins. It was not long before Rollo and Charles came in sight of one. The coachman was looking toward them, and was cracking his whip to attract their attention.

Rollo and Charles walked directly towards the spot, and Rollo, taking out his watch, and showing the coachman what o'clock it was, said,—

"*Per hora.*"

This was to notify the coachman that he took the carriage by the hour.

"*Si, signore,*" said the coachman; and then Rollo and Charles got in.

The carriage was entirely open,—the top being turned

back,—so that it afforded an uninterrupted view in every direction; and also, by standing up and pointing forward, the boys could easily indicate to the coachman which way they wished him to drive. Rollo, however, in the first instance, directed him in words to drive to the Corso.

"*Si, signore*," said the coachman; and so he drove on.

The boys sat in the carriage, or stood up to look back at the various objects of interest that attracted them as they passed. The scenes through which the driver took them seemed very strange. Every thing in Rome was strange to them, and their course now lay through a part of the city which they had not been in before. Their attention was continually attracted first upon this side of the carriage and then upon the other, as they rode along; and they pointed out to each other the remarkable objects they were passing.

The driver meanwhile upon his seat drove on, entirely indifferent to it all. The scenes that were so new to the boys, were perfectly familiar to him.

He soon entered a region of dark, crooked, and winding alleys, where Rollo said that he and Charles could never have found their way, if they had undertaken it alone. They frequently passed portions of old ruins. In some places these ruins consisted of columns standing alone, or immense fragments of broken arches that had fallen down, and now lay neglected upon the ground. In other places, the remains of ancient temples stood built in with the houses of the street, with market women at their stalls below, forming a strange and incongruous spectacle of ancient magnificence and splendor, surrounded and overwhelmed with modern poverty and degradation. As the carriage drove through these places, Rollo and Charles stood up in it, supporting themselves by pressing their knees against the front seat, and holding on to each other. They stood up thus partly to be enabled to see better, and partly so as to be ready to point out the way as soon as they should enter the Corso.

It was not long before they came to the Corso. The coachman then looked round, as if to inquire of the boys what he was to do next.

"Go right on," said Rollo; and so saying, he stood up in the carriage, and pointed forward. The coachman, of course, did not understand the words, but the gesture was significant enough, and so he drove on.

"Now watch, Charley, sharp," said Rollo; "and when you see the street that you think is the one where we came into the Corso, tell me."

So the boys drove on through the Corso, standing up all the time in the middle of the carriage, and looking about them in a very eager manner.

They went on in this way for some time, but they could not identify any of the branch streets as the one by which they had come into the Corso.

"Never mind," said Rollo; "we will turn off into any of these streets, and perhaps we shall come upon the hotel. We will take the streets that look most like it, and at any rate, we shall have a good ride, and see the city of Rome."

Rollo accordingly pointed to a side street when he wished the coachman to turn. The coachman said, "*Si, signore,*" and immediately went in that direction. As he advanced in the new street, the boys looked about on all sides to see if they could recognize any signs of their approach to their hotel.

After going on a little way, and seeing nothing that looked at all familiar, Rollo made signs to the coachman to turn down another street, which he thought looked promising. The coachman did as he was directed, wondering a little, however, at the strange demeanor of the boys; and feeling somewhat curious to know where they wanted to go. He, however, felt comparatively little interest in the question, after all; for, as he was paid by the hour, it was of no consequence to him where they directed him to drive.

Rollo now perceived that Charles began to be somewhat anxious in respect to the situation they were in, and so he tried in every way to encourage him, and to amuse his mind.

"I'll tell you what we will do," said Rollo. "This street that we are in now seems to be a good long one, and we will drive through the whole length of it, and you shall look down all the streets that open into it on the right hand, and I will on the left; and if we see any thing that looks like our hotel, we will stop."

So they rode on, each boy looking out on his side, until at length they came to the end of the street, where there was a sort of opening, and a river. There was a bridge across the river, and an ancient and venerable-looking castle on the other side of it.

"Ah," said Rollo, "here is the River Tiber."

"How do you know that that is the name of it?" asked Charles.

"Because I know it is the Tiber that Rome is built upon," replied Rollo,—"the Yellow Tiber, as they call it. Don't you see how yellow it is?"

As Rollo said this, he made signs for the coachman to turn out to the side of the street at the entrance of the bridge, and to stop there. The coachman did as he was directed, and then Rollo and Charles, still standing up in the carriage, had a fine view of the bridge and of the river, and also of the Castle of St. Angelo beyond. The water of the river was quite turbid, and was of a yellow color.

"That's the river," said Rollo, "that Romulus and Remus were floated down on, in that little ark."

"What little ark?" asked Charles.

"Why, you see," replied Rollo, "when Romulus and Remus were babies, the story is that somebody wanted to have them killed; but he did not like to kill them himself with his own hand, and therefore he put them into a sort of basket, made of bulrushes, and set them afloat on this river, up above here a little way. So they floated down the stream, and came along by here."

"Under this bridge?" asked Charles.

"Under where this bridge is now," said Rollo; "but of course there was no bridge here then. There was no town here then—nothing but fields and woods."

"And what became of the babies?" asked Charles.

"Why, they floated down below here a little way," said Rollo, "to a place where there is a turn in the river; and there the basket went ashore, and was upset, and the children crawled out on the sand, and began to cry. Pretty soon a wolf, who was in the thicket near by, heard the crying, and came down to see what it was."

"And did he eat them up?" asked Charles.

"It was not a he wolf," said Rollo; "it was a she wolf—an old mother wolf. She thought that the children were little wolves, and she came to them, and lay down by them, nursed them, and took care of them, just as if she had been a cat, and they had been her two kittens."

"O Rollo," said Charles, "what a story! I don't believe it."

"Nor I," said Rollo. "Indeed, I don't think any body nowadays believes it exactly. But that is really the story. You can read it in the history of Rome. These two children, when they grew up, laid the foundations of Rome. I don't really believe that the story is true; but if it is true, this is the very place where the basket, with the two babies in it, must have drifted along."

Charles gazed for a few minutes in silence on the current of turbid water which was shooting swiftly under the bridge, and then said that it was time for them to go.

"Yes," said Rollo; "and we will turn round and go back, for it is of no use to go over the bridge. I am sure that we did not come over the river when we set out from the hotel, and so we must keep on this side."

Rollo concluded, however, not to go back the same way that he came; and so making signs to the coachman for this purpose, he turned into another street, and as the carriage drove along, he and Charles looked out in every direction for their hotel; but no signs of it were to be seen.

After going on for some distance, Rollo's attention was attracted by a sign in English over a shop door as follows:—

MANUFACTURE OF ROMAN SCARFS. ENGLISH SPOKEN.

"Ah!" he exclaimed, suddenly, "that is just what I wanted to find." And he immediately made a sign for the coachman to stop at the door.

"What is it?" asked Charles.

"It is a place where they make Roman scarfs," said Rollo, "and I want to get one for my cousin Lucy. She told me to be sure, if I came to Rome, to get her a Roman scarf. You can't get them in any other place."

As Rollo said this, he descended from the carriage, and Charles followed him.

"They speak English here," said Rollo, as he went into the shop, "and so we shall not have any difficulty."

These Roman scarfs are very pretty ornaments for the necks and shoulders of ladies. They are made of silk, and are of various sizes, some being large enough to form a good wide mantle, and others not much wider than a wide ribbon. The central part of the scarf is usually of some uniform hue, such as black, blue, green, or brown; and the ends are ornamented with stripes of various colors, which pass across from side to side.

Rollo wished to get a small scarf, and the ground of it was to be green. This was in accordance with the instructions which Lucy had given him. He found great difficulty, however, in making the shopman understand what he wanted. To all that Rollo said, the shopman smiled, and said only, "Yes, sir, yes, sir," and took down continually scarfs and aprons of different kinds, and showed them to Rollo, to see if any of them were what he wanted.

At last, by pointing to a large one that had a green ground, and saying, "Color like that," and then to a small one of a different kind, and saying, "Small, like that," the shopman began to understand.

"Yes, sir," said the shopman; "yes, sir; I understand. Must one make—make. See!"

So saying, the shopman opened a door in the back side of the shop, and showed Rollo and Charles the entrance to a room in the rear, where the boys had heard before the sound of a continual thumping, and where now they saw several silk looms, with girls at work at them, weaving scarfs.

"Ah, yes," said Rollo. "You mean that you can make me one. That will be a good plan, Charley," he added. "Lucy will like it all the better if I tell her it was made on purpose for her.

"When can you have it done?" asked Rollo.

"Yes, sir," said the shopman, bowing and smiling; "yes, sir; yes, sir."

"When?" repeated Rollo. "What time?"

"Ah, yes, sir," said the shopman. "The time. All time, every time. Yesterday."

"Yesterday!" repeated Rollo, puzzled.

"To-morrow," said the man, correcting himself. He had said yesterday by mistake for to-morrow. "To-morrow. To-morrow he will be ready—the scarf."

"What time to-morrow shall I come?" asked Rollo.

"Yes, sir," said the shopman, bowing again, and smiling in a very complacent manner. "Yes, sir, to-morrow."

"But what *time* to-morrow?" repeated Rollo, speaking very distinctly, and emphasizing very strongly the word *time*. "What time?"

"O, every time," said the man; "all time. You shall have him every time to-morrow, because you see he will make begin the work on him this day."

"Very well," said Rollo, "then I will come to-morrow, about noon."

So Rollo and Charles bade the shopman good by, and went out of the shop.

"Is that what they call speaking English?" asked Charles.

"So it seems," said Rollo. "Sometimes they speak a great deal worse than that, and yet call it speaking English."

So Rollo and Charles got into the carriage again. Rollo took out his wallet, and made a memorandum of the name of the shop where he had engaged the sash, and of the street and number. The coachman sat quietly upon his seat, waiting for Rollo to finish his writing, and expecting then to receive directions where he was to go.

"If I could only find a commissioner that speaks French or English," said Rollo, "I could tell him what we want, and he could tell the coachman, and in that way we should soon get home."

"Can't you find one at some hotel?" asked Charles.

"Why, yes," said Rollo. "Why did not I think of that? We'll stop at the very first hotel we come to. I'll let him drive on till he comes to one. No; I'll tell him to go to the Hotel d'Amerique. That is the only name of a hotel that I know."

So Rollo pronounced the words "Hotel d'Amerique" to the coachman, and the coachman, saying, "*Si, signore*," drove on. In a short time he drew up before the door of the hotel where Mr. George had stopped first, on arriving in town. A waiter came to the door.

"Is there a commissioner here who speaks English or French?" asked Rollo.

"Yes, sir," said a man who was standing by the side of the door when the carriage stopped, and who now came forward. "*I* speak English."

"I want you to help us find our hotel," said Rollo. "We don't know the name of it. I shall know it when I see it; and so I want you to get on the box with the coachman, and direct him to drive to one hotel after another, till I see which is the right one."

"Very well," said the commissioner, "I will go. Do you remember any thing about the hotel,—how it was situated."

"There was a small, open space before it," said Rollo, "and a fountain under a tree by the side of it."

"It must have been the Hotel d'Angleterre," said the commissioner.

"In going in at the front door, we went *down* one or two steps, instead of up," said Rollo.

"Yes," said the commissioner, "it was the Hotel d'Angleterre." Then seating himself on the box by the side of the coachman, he said to the latter, addressing him in Italian,—

"Lo canda d'Ingleterra," which is the Italian for Hotel d'Angleterre, or, as we should express it in our language, "The English Hotel."

The coachman drove on, and in a few minutes came to the hotel.

"Yes," said Rollo, as soon as he came in sight of it. "Yes, this is the very place."

If Rollo had had any doubts of his being right, they would have been dispelled by the sight of Mr. George, who was standing at the hotel door at the time they arrived.

"So you come home in a carriage," said Mr. George.

"Why, we got lost," said Rollo. "I did not take notice of the name of our hotel when we went out, and so we could not find our way home again."

"That's of no consequence," said Mr. George. "I am glad you had sense enough to take a commissioner. Whenever you get into any difficulty whatever in a European town, go right to a commissioner, and he will help you out."

So Rollo paid the coachman and the commissioner, and then he and Charles went into the hotel.

Jacob Abbott

CHAPTER VI

THE COLISEUM

The grandest of all the ruins in Rome, and perhaps, indeed, of all the ruins in the world, is the Coliseum.

The Coliseum was built as a place for the exhibition of games and spectacles. It was of an oval form, with seats rising one above another on all sides, and a large arena in the centre. There was no roof. The building was so immensely large, that it would have been almost impossible to have made a roof over it.

The spectacles which were exhibited in such buildings as these were usually combats, either of men with men, or of men with wild beasts. These were real combats, in which either the men or the beasts were actually killed. The thousands of people that sat upon the seats all around, watched the conflict, while it was going on, with intense excitement, and shouted with ferocious joy at the end of it, in honor of the victors.

The men that fought in the arena were generally captives taken in battle, in distant countries, and the wild beasts were lions, tigers, and bears, that were sent home from Africa, or from the dark forests in the north of Europe.

The great generals who went out at the head of the Roman armies to conquer these distant realms and annex them to the empire, sent home these captives and wild beasts. They sent them for the express purpose of amusing the Roman people with them, by making them fight in these great amphitheatres. There was such an amphitheatre in or near almost every large town; but the greatest, or at least the most celebrated, of all these structures, was this Coliseum at Rome.

Mr. George and Rollo went to the Coliseum in a carriage. After passing through almost the whole length of the Corso, they passed successively through several crooked and narrow streets, and at length emerged into the great region of the ruins. On every side were tall columns, broken and decayed, and immense arches standing meaningless and alone, and mounds of ancient masonry, with weeds and flowers waving in the air on the top of them. There were no houses, or scarcely any, in this part of the city, but only grassy slopes with old walls appearing here and there among them; and in some places enclosed fields and gardens, with corn, and beans, and garden vegetables of every kind, growing at the base of the majestic ruins.

The carriage stopped at one end of the Coliseum, where there was a passage way leading through stupendous arches into the interior.

They dismissed the carriage, Rollo having first paid the coachman the fare. They then, after gazing upward a moment at the vast pile of arches upon arches, towering above them, advanced towards the openings, in order to go in.

There was a soldier with a musket in his hands, bayonet

set, walking to and fro at the entrance. He, however, said nothing to Mr. George and Rollo; and so, passing by him, they went in.

They passed in under immense arches of the most massive masonry, and between the great piers built to sustain the arches, until they reached the arena. There was a broad gravel walk passing across the arena from end to end, and another leading around the circumference of it. The rest of the surface was covered with grass, smooth and green.

The form of the arena was oval, as has already been said, and on every side there ascended the sloping tiers, rising one above another to a vast height, on which the seats for the spectators had been placed. Mr. George and Rollo advanced along the central walk, and looked around them, surveying the scene,—their minds filled with emotions of wonder and awe.

"What a monstrous place it was!" said Rollo.

"It was, indeed," said Mr. George.

"Is it here where the men fought with the lions and the tigers?" asked Rollo, pointing around him over the arena.

"Yes," said Mr. George.

"And up there, all around were the seats of the spectators, I suppose," said Rollo.

"Yes," said Mr. George, "on those slopes."

You must know that the scats, and all the inside finish of the Coliseum, were originally of marble, and people have stripped it all away, and left nothing but the naked masonry; and even that is all now going to ruin.

"What did they strip the marble off for?" asked Rollo.

"To build their houses and palaces with," replied Mr. George. "Half of the modern palaces of Rome are built of stone and marble plundered from the ancient ruins."

"O, uncle George!" exclaimed Rollo.

"Come out here where we can sit down," said Mr. George, "and I'll tell you all about it."

So saying, Mr. George led the way, and Rollo followed to one side of the arena, where they could sit down on a large, flat stone, which seemed to have been an ancient step. They were over-shadowed where they sat by piers and arches, and by the masses of weeds and shrubbery that were growing on the mouldering summits of them, and waving in the wind.

In the centre of the arena was a large cross, with a sort of platform around it, and steps to go up. And all around the arena, on the sides, at equal distances, there extended a range of little chapels, with crucifixes and other Catholic symbols.

The arena of the Coliseum was kept in very neat order. For a wonder, there were no beggars to be seen, but instead of them there were various parties of well-dressed visitors walking about the paths, or sitting on the massive stone fragments which lay under the ruined arches.

High up above these arches, the sloping platforms, on which the seats formerly were placed, were to be seen

Jacob Abbott

rising one above another, tier after tier, to a great height, with the ruins of galleries, corridors, and vaulted passage ways passing around among them. The upper surfaces of all these ruins were covered with grass and shrubbery.

"What has become of all the seats, uncle George?" said Rollo.

"Why, the seats, I suppose, were made of marble," replied Mr. George. "or some other valuable material, and so all the stones have been taken away."

Presently Rollo saw a party of visitors coming into view far up among the upper stories of the ruins.

"Look, uncle George! Look!" said he; "there are some people away up there, as high as the third or fourth story. How do you suppose they got up there? Couldn't you and I go?"

"I presume so," said Mr. George. "I suppose that, in the way of climbing, you and I can go as high as most people."

While Mr. George was saying this, Rollo was adjusting his opera glass to his eyes, in order to take a nearer view of the party among the ruins.

"There are four of them," said he. "I see a gentleman, and two ladies, and a little girl. They seem to be gathering something."

"Plants, perhaps," said Mr. George, "and flowers."

"Plants!" said Rollo, contemptuously; "I don't believe that any thing grows out of such old stones and mortar but weeds."

"We call such things weeds," said Mr. George, "when they grow in the gardens or fields, and are in the way; but when they grow in wild places where they belong, they are plants and flowers."

"The gentleman is gathering them from high places all around him," said Rollo, "and is giving them to the ladies, and they are putting them in between the leaves of a book."

"They are going to carry them away as souvenirs of the Coliseum, I suppose," said Mr. George.

"The girl has got a white stone in her hand," said Rollo.

"Perhaps it is a piece of marble that she has picked up," said Mr. George.

"Now she has thrown down her white stone," said Rollo, "and has begun to gather flowers."

"There is an immense number of plants that grow in and upon the Coliseum," said Mr. George. "A botanist once made a complete collection of them. How many species do you think he found?"

"Twenty," said Rollo.

"Guess again," said Mr. George.

"Fifteen," said Rollo.

"O, you must guess more, not less," said Mr. George.

"Thirty," said Rollo.

"More," said Mr. George.

"Forty," said Rollo.

"Add one cipher to it," said Mr. George, "and then you will be pretty near right."

"What! four hundred?" exclaimed Rollo.

"Yes," said Mr. George. "A botanist made a catalogue of four hundred and twenty plants, all growing on the ruins of this single building."

"O, uncle George!" said Rollo; "I don't think that can possibly be. I mean to see."

So saying, Rollo laid the opera glass down upon the seat where he had been sitting, and began to examine the masses of old ruined masonry near him, with a view of seeing how many different kinds of plants he could find.

"Must I court every thing, uncle George?" said Rollo.

"Yes," said Mr. George, "every thing that is a plant. Every different kind of sprig, or little weed, that you can find—mosses, lichens, and all."

Rollo began to count. He very soon got up to twenty, and so he came to the conclusion that the guide book—which was the authority on which Mr. George had stated the number of plants found upon the ruins—was right.

While Rollo was thus engaged, Mr. George had remained quietly in his seat, and had occupied himself with studying the guide book.

"Uncle George," said Rollo, when he came back, "I give it up. I have no doubt that there are hundreds of plants in all, growing on these ruins."

"Yes," said Mr. George; "whatever is stated in this book is very apt to prove true."

"What else did you read about, uncle George," said Rollo, "while I was counting the plants?"

"I read," said Mr. George, "that the Coliseum was begun about A. D. 72, by one of the Roman emperors."

"Then it is almost eighteen hundred years old," said Rollo.

"Yes," said Mr. George; "and when it was first opened after it was finished, they had a sort of inauguration of it, with great celebrations, that continued one hundred days."

"That is over three months," said Rollo.

"Yes," said Mr. George; "it was a very long celebration. During this time about five thousand wild beasts were killed in the combats in the arena."

"This very arena right before us?" said Rollo.

"Yes," said Mr. George.

On hearing this, Rollo looked upon the arena with renewed interest and pleasure. He endeavored to picture to himself the lions, and tigers, and leopards, and other ferocious wild beasts, growling, snarling, and tumbling over each other there, in the desperate combats which they waged among themselves, or with the men sent in to fight with them.

"It continued to be used for such fights," added Mr. George, "for four hundred years; and during this time a great many Christians were sent in to be devoured by wild beasts, for the entertainment of the populace.

"After a while," continued Mr. George, "the Roman empire became Christian; and then the government put a stop to all these savage games."

"And what did they do with the Coliseum then?" asked Rollo.

"They did not know what to do with it for a time," said Mr. George; "but at last, when wars broke out, and Rome was besieged, they tried to turn it into a fortress."

"I should think it would make an excellent fortress," said Rollo, "only there are no port-holes for the cannon."

"Ah! but they had no cannon in those days," said Mr. George. "They had only bows and arrows, spears, javelins, and such sort of weapons, so that they did not require any port-holes. The men could shoot their weapons from the top of the wall."

In further conversation on the subject of the Coliseum, Mr. George explained to Rollo how, in process of time, Rome was taken by the barbarians, and a great portion of the Coliseum was destroyed; and then, afterwards, when peace was restored, how the government, instead of repairing the building, pulled it to pieces still more, in order to get marble, and hewn stone, and sculptured columns, to build palaces with; and how, at a later period, there was a plan formed for converting the vast structure into a manufactory; and how, in connection with this plan, immense numbers of shops were fitted up in the arcades and arches below,—and how the plan finally failed, after having cost the pope who undertook it ever so many thousand Roman dollars; how, after this, it remained for many centuries wholly neglected, and the stones, falling in from above, together with the broken bricks and mortar, formed on the arena below, and all around the walls outside, immense heaps of rubbish; and finally, how, about one hundred years ago, people began to take an interest in the ruins, and to wish to clear away the rubbish, and to prop up and preserve what remained of the walls and arches.

"It was the French that cleared away the rubbish at last," said Mr. George, "and put the ruins in order."

"The French!" repeated Rollo; "how came the French here?"

"I don't know," said Mr. George. "The French are every where. And wherever they go, they always take with their armies a corps of philosophers, artists, and men of science, who look up every thing that is curious, and put it in order, and preserve it if they can."

"Then I am glad they came here," said Rollo.

Here Mr. George shut his book, and rose from his seat, saying, as he did so,—

"The Coliseum is so large that it covers six acres of ground."

"Six acres?" repeated Rollo.

Jacob Abbott

"Yes," said Mr. George. "It is six hundred and twenty feet long. That is monstrous for such a building; but then the steamship Great Eastern is about a hundred feet longer."

"Then the Great Eastern is bigger than the Coliseum."

"She is longer," said Mr. George, "but she is not so wide nor so high."

"And which, all things considered, is the greatest work, do you think?" asked Rollo.

"The Coliseum may have cost the most labor," said Mr. George, "but the Great Eastern is far above it, in my opinion, in every element of real greatness. The Coliseum is a most wonderful structure, no doubt; but the building of an iron ship like the Great Eastern, to be propelled by steam against all the storms and tempests of the ocean, to the remotest corners of the earth, with ten thousand tons of merchandise on board, or ten thousand men, is, in my opinion, much the greatest exploit."

"At any rate," said Rollo, "the Coliseum makes the finest ruin."

"I am not certain of that, even," said Mr. George. "Suppose that the Great Eastern were to be drawn up upon the shore somewhere near London, and be abandoned there; and that then the whole world should relapse into barbarism, and remain so for a thousand years, and afterwards there should come a revival of science and civilization, and people should come here to see the ruins of the Coliseum, and go to London to see those of the great ship, I think they would consider the ship the greater wonder of the two."

"I think they would," said Rollo, "if they understood it all as well."

"They could not be easily made to believe, I suppose," said Mr. George, "that such an immense structure, all of iron, could have been made, and launched, and then navigated all over the world just by the power of the maze of iron beams and wheels, and machinery, which they would see in ruins in the hold."

"Uncle George," said Rollo, "what curious bricks the Romans used!"

So saying, Rollo pointed to the bricks in a mass of masonry near where they were standing. These bricks, like all those that were used in the construction of the building, were very flat. They were a great deal longer and a great deal wider than our bricks, and were yet not much more than half as thick. This gave them a very thin and flat appearance. Instead of being red, too, they were of a yellow color.

These bricks had not originally been used for outside works, but only for filling in the solid parts of the walls, and for forming the arches. But the stones with which the brick masonry had been covered and concealed having been removed, the bricks were of course in many places brought to view.

After looking about for some time, Rollo found a brick with two letters stamped upon it. It was evident that the letters had been stamped upon the clay in the making of the brick, while it was yet soft. The letters were P. D.

"Look, uncle George!" said Rollo; "look at those letters! What do you suppose they mean?"

"That is very curious," said Mr. George; and so saying he proceeded to examine the letters very closely.

"They were evidently stamped upon the brick," he said, "when it was soft. Perhaps they are the initials of the maker's name."

"I mean to look and see if all the bricks are stamped so," said Rollo.

So Rollo began to examine the other bricks wherever he could find any which had a side exposed to view; but though he found some which contained the letters, there were many others where no letters were to be seen.

"Perhaps the letters are on the under side," said Rollo. "I mean to get a stone and knock up some of the bricks, if I can, and see."

"No," said Mr. George; "that won't do."

"Yes, uncle George," said Rollo; "I want to see very much. And besides, I want to get a piece of a brick with the letters on it, to carry home as a specimen."

"A specimen of what?" asked Mr. George.

"A specimen of the Coliseum," said Rollo.

"No," said Mr. George; "I don't think that will do. They don't want to have the Coliseum knocked to pieces, and carried off any more."

"Who don't? ' asked Rollo.

"The government," said Mr. George; "the pope."

"But it's very hard," said Rollo, "if the popes, after plundering the Coliseum themselves for hundreds of years, and carrying off all the beautiful marbles, and columns, and statues, to build their palaces with, can't let an American boy like me take away a little bit of a brick to put into my museum for a specimen."

Mr. George laughed and walked on. Rollo, who never persisted in desiring to do any thing which his uncle disapproved of, quietly followed him.

"Uncle George," said Rollo, "how do you suppose we can get up into the upper part, among the tiers of seats?"

"I think there must be a staircase somewhere," said Mr. George. "We will ramble about, and see if we do not find one."

So they walked on. They went sometimes along the margin of the arena, and then at other times they turned in under immense openings in masonry, and walked along the vaulted corridors, which were built in the thickness of the walls. There were several of these corridors side by side, each going entirely round the arena. They were surmounted by stupendous arches, which were built to sustain the upper portions of the building, which contained the seats for the spectators, and the passages on the upper floors leading to them.

After rambling on through and among the corridors for some time, Mr. George and Rollo, on emerging again into the arena, came to a wooden gate at the foot of a broad flight of stone steps, which seemed to lead up into the higher stories of the ruin.

"Ah!" exclaimed Rollo, as soon as he saw this gateway

Jacob Abbott

and the flight of steps beyond it, "this is the gate that leads up to the upper tiers."

"Yes," replied Mr. George, "only it is shut and locked."

Rollo went to the gate and took hold of it, but found, as Mr. George had said, that it was locked.

"But here comes the custodian," said Mr. George.

Rollo looked, and saw a man coming along the side of the arena with a key in his hand. When the man came near, he looked at Mr. George and Rollo, and also at the door, and then asked a question in Italian.

"*Si, signore*,' said Mr. George.

So the man advanced and unlocked the door. As soon as he had unlocked it, and Mr. George and Rollo had passed through, he looked towards them again, and asked another question.

"*No, signore*," said Mr. George.

Mr. George and Rollo then began to go up the stairs, while the man, having locked the door after them, went away.

CHAPTER VII

THE GLADIATOR

"How did you know what it was that that man asked you?" asked Rollo.

"I knew from the circumstances of the case," replied Mr. George. "The first question I knew must be whether we wished to go up; and the second, whether we wished him to go with us."

"What do you suppose they keep the gate locked for?" asked Rollo.

"So as to *make* us pay when we come down," said Mr. George.

"Do you suppose they mean to make us pay?" asked Rollo.

"They will not make us, exactly," said Mr. George; "but they will expect something, no doubt. There may be another reason, however, why they keep the gate locked; and that is, to prevent children and stragglers from going up, where they might fall and break their necks at some of the exposed and dangerous places."

"Do you suppose that there are dangerous places up here?" asked Rollo.

"Yes," said Mr. George; "I suppose there are a great many; and I advise you to be very careful where you go."

The flight of stairs where Mr. George and Rollo were ascending was very broad; and it was formed of the long, flat bricks, such as Rollo had observed below. The bricks were placed edgewise.

"I suppose that these steps were covered with slabs of marble, in old times," said Rollo.

"Probably," said Mr. George; "either with marble, or some other harder stone."

After ascending some distance, Rollo, who went forward, came out upon the landing which led to a range of corridors in the second story, as it were. There were several of these corridors, running side by side, all along the building. On one side, you could pass through arches, and come out to the platforms where the seats had originally been arranged, and where you could look down upon the arena. The seats themselves were all gone, and in their places nothing was left but sloping platforms, all gone to ruin, and covered now with grass, and weeds, and tall bramble bushes. On the other side, you could go out to the outer wall, and look down through immense arched openings, to the ground below.[5]

[Footnote 5: See Frontispiece.]

"Take care, Rollo," said Mr. George; "don't go too near."

"You may go as near as you think it is safe," said Rollo,

"and I will keep back an inch from where you go."

"That's right," said Mr. George. "There is great pleasure and satisfaction in going into dangerous places with such a sensible boy as you."

After rambling about among the arches and corridors of the second story for some time, Mr. George and Rollo mounted to a story above. They found ruins of staircases in great numbers, so that there were a great many different places where they could go up. Mr. George allowed Rollo to go about wherever he pleased, knowing that he would keep at a safe distance from all places where there was danger of falling.

From time to time, they met other parties of visitors rambling about the ruins. If these persons were French or German, they generally bowed to Rollo and Mr. George as they passed, and greeted them with a pleasant smile, as if of recognition. If, on the other hand, they were English, they passed directly by, looking straight forward, as if they did not see them at all.

Whenever Rollo came to a new staircase, he wished to ascend it, being seemingly desirous of getting up as high as he could. Mr. George made no objection to this. Indeed, he allowed Rollo to choose the way, and to go where he pleased. He himself followed, walking slowly, in a musing manner, filled, apparently, with wondering admiration, and contemplating the stupendous magnitude of the ruin.

"Uncle George," said Rollo, "if I had my pressing book here, I would gather some of these plants and press them, to carry home."

Mr. George did not answer. He was standing in an advanced position, where he had an uninterrupted survey of the whole interior of the Coliseum; and he was endeavoring to picture to his imagination the scene which must have been presented to view when the vast amphitheatre was filled with spectators.

"If I had expected to find so many plants growing on the ruins of a building, I should have brought it," said Rollo.

The pressing book which Rollo referred to, was one made expressly for the purpose of pressing flowers. The leaves of it were of blotting paper.

Rollo was half inclined to ask Mr. George to put some specimens into the Guide Book; but he did *not* ask him, because he knew that Mr. George did not like to have dried plants in the Guide Book. Such specimens between the leaves of a book interfere very much with the convenience of using it, by dropping out when you open the book, or impeding the turning of the leaves.

"But I mean to come again," continued Rollo, "and bring my pressing book, and then I can get as many specimens as I please. Wouldn't you, uncle George?"

"Wouldn't you what?" said Mr. George. Mr. George had been paying very little attention to what Rollo had been saying.

"Come again some day," said Rollo, "and bring my pressing book, so as to collect specimens of some of these little plants.'

"Yes," said Mr. George, "that will be an excellent plan. And I wish, while you are doing it, you would gather some for me. And if you wish for some now, I can let you put them in the Guide Book."

"No, I thank you," said Rollo. "I will wait till I come again."

The height of the outer walls of the Coliseum is over a hundred and fifty feet, which would be the height of a house fifteen stories high. There are not many church steeples higher than that.

If, therefore, you conceive of an oval-shaped field six acres in extent, with a massive wall one hundred and fifty feet high, and divided into four immense stories, surrounding it, and from the top of this wall ranges of seats, with passages between them, sloping in towards the centre, leaving about an acre of open and level space in the centre for the arena, the whole finished in the most magnificent and gorgeous manner, with columns, statues, sculptured ornaments, and all the seats, and walls, and staircases, and corridors, and vestibules, and tribunes, and pavilions for musicians, and seats for judges, designed and arranged in the highest style of architectural beauty, and encased and adorned with variegated marbles of the most gorgeous description,—if, I say, you can conceive of all this, you will have some faint idea of what the Coliseum must have been in the days of its glory.

Mr. George and Rollo continued to ascend the different staircases which they met with in their wanderings, until at length they had reached a great elevation; and yet so immense was the extent of the interior of the edifice, that they were not at all too high to see the arena to advantage. Here Rollo crept out upon one of the sloping platforms, where there had formerly been seats for spectators, and calling to Mr. George to follow him, he sat down upon a great square stone, which seemed to have formed a part of the ancient foundation of the seats.

"Come, uncle George," said Rollo, "let us sit down here a few minutes, and make believe that the games are going on, and that we are the spectators."

"Yes," said Mr. George, "we will. In that way we can get a better idea of what the Coliseum was."

"I wish we could bring it all back again," said Rollo, "just as it was in old times, by some sort of magic."

"We must do it by the magic of imagination," said Mr. George.

"Only," continued Rollo, "the things that they did down in the arena were so dreadful that we could not bear to look at them."

"True," said Mr. George. "The spectacles must have been very dreadful, indeed."

"Such as when the lions and tigers came out to tear and devour the poor Christians," said Rollo.

"Yes," said Mr. George; "but generally, I suppose, when wild beasts and men were brought out together on the arena, it was the beasts that were killed, and not the men. It was a combat, and I suppose that the men were usually victorious. It was the spectacle of the fury of the combat, and of the bravery which the men displayed, and of the terrible danger that they were often exposed to, that so excited and pleased the spectators."

"I should not have thought that they could have found any

men that would have been willing to fight the beasts," said Rollo.

"Perhaps the men were not willing," replied Mr. George, "but were compelled to fight them. Indeed, I suppose that they were generally prisoners of war or criminals. The generals used to bring home a great many prisoners of war from the different countries that they conquered, and these men were trained in Rome, and in other great cities, to fight on the arena, either with wild beasts, or with one another. They were called *gladiators*. There is a statue of one, wounded and dying, somewhere here in Rome."

"I should like to see it," said Rollo.

"We *shall* see it, undoubtedly," said Mr. George. "It is one of the most celebrated statues in the world. It is called the *Dying Gladiator*. I presume the sculptor of it made it from his recollections of the posture and expression of face which were witnessed in the case of real gladiators in the arena, when they had been mortally wounded, and were sinking down to die."

"We certainly must see it," said Rollo.

"We certainly will," rejoined Mr. George. "It is celebrated all over the world. Byron wrote a very fine stanza describing it."

"What was the stanza?" asked Rollo.

"I don't remember it all," said Mr. George. "It was something about his sinking down upon the ground, leaning upon his hand, and the expression of his face showed, though he yielded to death, he conquered and triumphed over the pain. Then there is something about his wife and children, far away in Dacia, his native land, where he had been captured in fighting to protect them, and brought to Rome to fight and die in the Coliseum, to make amusement for the Roman populace."

"I wish you could remember the lines themselves," said Rollo.

"Perhaps I can find them in the Guide Book," said Mr. George.

So saying, Mr. George opened the Guide Book, and turned to the index.

"I believe," said he, "that the statue of the Dying Gladiator is in the Capitol."

"We have not been there yet, have we?" asked Rollo.

"Yes," replied Mr. George; "we went there the first day, to get a view from the cupola on the summit. But there is a museum of sculptures and statues there which we have not seen yet. You see the Capitol Hill was in ancient times one of the most important public places in Rome, and when the city was destroyed, immense numbers of statues, and inscribed marbles, and beautiful sculptured ornaments were buried up there in the rubbish and ruins. When, finally, they were dug out, new buildings were erected on the spot, and all the objects that were found there were arranged in a museum. Ah! here it is," he added. "I have found the lines."

So Mr. George read the lines as follows. He read them in a slow and solemn manner.

"I see before me the gladiator lie;

He leans upon his hand; his manly brow
Consents to death, but conquers agony;
And his drooped head sinks gradually low;
And through his side the last drops, ebbing slow
From the red gash, fall heavy, one by one,
Like the first of a thunder shower; and now
The arena swims around him—he is gone,
Ere ceased the inhuman shout which hailed the wretch
who won.

"He heard it, but he heeded not; his eyes
Were with his heart, and that was far away.
He recked not of the life he lost, nor prize,
But where his rude hut by the Danube lay,
There were his young barbarians all at play;
There was their Dacian mother—he, their sire,
Butchered to make a Roman holiday.
All this rushed with his blood. Shall he expire,
And unavenged? Arise, ye Goths, and glut your ire."

"The Goths did arise and glut their ire," said Mr. George, after he had finished reciting the lines, "for they were in great measure the authors of all this ruin and destruction."

After sitting nearly half an hour in this place, Mr. George rose, and, Rollo following him, went back into the corridors again. They rambled along the corridors, and mounted the staircases to higher and higher points, until they had ascended as far as they could go. In these upper regions of the ruin Rollo had a good opportunity to procure specimens of marble and of stamped bricks, for in various places there, he found immense stores of bricks and marble, and other rubbish, piled up in square heaps under arches, or in great recesses among the ruins. Rollo selected some of the bricks which had stamps upon them, and then, with a piece of marble for a hammer, he contrived to break away all of the brick except the part which contained the stamp, and thus procured specimens of a convenient form for carrying. These specimens he wrapped separately in pieces of newspaper, and put them in his pockets.

At length Mr. George said it was time for them to go home; so they began to descend. They went down by different passages and staircases from those which they had taken in coming up; but they came out at last at the same gateway. The custodian was just unlocking the gate when they arrived, in order to admit another party. Mr. George gave him a couple of pauls, and then he and Rollo set out to go home.

Their way led them over the ancient site of the Roman Forum, which presented to view on every side, as they passed, broken columns and ruined arches, with the mouldering remains of ancient foundations, cropping out here and there amid grassy slopes and mounds.

"Uncle George," said Rollo, as they walked along, "we are going directly by the Capitol Hill as we go home. Let us go in now and see the Dying Gladiator."

"Very well," said Mr. George, "we will."

Accordingly, when they reached the base of the hill, they turned to go up. There was a broad and steep paved ascent leading up the hill, somewhat like a road, only it was too steep for a carriage. Indeed, there were little steps at short intervals, with a sloping pavement between them. You see this ascent in the engraving. It is in the centre of the view. There are statues of lions at the foot of it, with water spouting from their mouths. At the top are larger statues of horses, standing on lofty pedestals, with men by the side of them, holding them by the bridles. These are ancient statues. They were found buried up in rubbish in an obscure quarter of Rome, about two hundred years ago. Beyond, you see other groups of colossal statuary raised on lofty pedestals in various parts of the great square which forms the summit of the hill.

On the left you see a church, standing in a very high position, with a still steeper ascent than the one I have been describing, leading up to it. On the right is a winding road for carriages, which leads up, by a tolerably gentle ascent, to the great square.

The great square is surrounded with vast palaces, almost all of which are filled with paintings, statuary, sculptures, and other treasures of ancient and modern art. Mr. George and Rollo turned to the left after they had ascended into the square, and entered a door over which was an inscription denoting that it led to the museum of sculptures and statues. After ascending one or two staircases, they came to the entrance of a suit of apartments in which the statuary was contained. There was a public functionary, dressed somewhat like a soldier, standing sentinel at the door. He, however, readily allowed Mr. George and Rollo to pass in. There were various other parties of visitors going in at the same time.

Mr. George and Rollo walked through one long room after another, with rows of statues, and busts, and other works of ancient sculpture on each side. These marbles were almost all more or less chipped and broken, or otherwise greatly defaced by the hard usage to which they had been subjected.

"Uncle George," said Rollo, as they walked along, "how came all their ears and noses broken off in this way?"

Jacob Abbott

"Why, all these things were dug out from heaps of stones and rubbish," said Mr. George, "a few hundred years ago. For nearly a thousand years before that time, they were regarded as of no more value than so many old bricks.

"Here's a gentleman coming," added Mr. George, interrupting himself, "who looks as if he could speak French. I mean to ask him where the hall of the Dying Gladiator is."

Accordingly, when the gentleman came up, Mr. George, accosting him in French, asked him the question, and the gentleman, replying in French, gave the information in a very polite manner. It was a little farther on, he said.

"Is there a special hall for the Dying Gladiator?" asked Rollo.

"No," said Mr. George, "not for the Dying Gladiator alone. But many of the halls in these museums are named from the most celebrated statue that there is in them. And I knew that the room where the Dying Gladiator is placed was called by that name."

So they walked on, and presently they came to the room. There were a great many large statues in it; but among them it was very easy to recognize at once the one which they had come to see, both on account of the conspicuous situation in which it was placed, and also from its form. Here is a representation of it.

Mr. George and Rollo both looked upon the statue for a few minutes in silence.

"Yes," said Rollo, at length, "yes, I see. He is dying. He is sinking gradually down."

"Do you see the wound in his side?" asked Mr. George.

"Yes," replied Rollo, "and the drops of blood coming out."

"He has dropped his sword," said Mr. George. "It is lying there near his hand."

"What a short sword!" said Rollo. "There are some other things lying on the ground beneath him, but I do not know what they are."

"Nor I," said Mr. George. "One of them seems to be a sort of trumpet. People think from that that this man was a herald."

"But I thought he was a gladiator," said Rollo.

"They call him a gladiator," replied Mr. George, "but nobody really knows what the statue was originally intended for. You see it was dug up out of a heap of rubbish, just as almost all these statues were, and people have to guess what they were intended for. This statue was dug up in a garden—a garden belonging to an ancient Roman villa."

"What does that cord around his neck mean?" asked Rollo.

"They think it means that the man was a Gaul. The Gauls used to wear such cords, I believe."

"I thought he was a Dacian," said Rollo.

"I suppose it is uncertain who he was," replied Mr. George; "but look at his face. See the expression of it. It is an expression of mingled suffering and rage, and yet he looks as if he were so far gone as to begin to be unconscious of every thing around him."

"Yes," said Rollo; "he does not seem to notice us at all."

"In that," said Mr. George, "is shown the great skill of the sculptor, to express such different, and, as one would think, almost conflicting emotions in the same face, at the same time."

After looking at the statue some time longer, Rollo and Mr. George walked around the room, and looked at the other pieces of sculpture that there were there. They afterwards came back again to the gladiator, in order to take one more view of it before they went away. Mr. George advised Rollo to look at it well, and impress the image of it strongly on his mind.

"It is one of the treasures of the world," said he; "and in the course of your life, though you may never see it here, in the original, again, you will meet with casts of it and drawings of it without number, and you will find descriptions of it and allusions to it continually recurring in the conversation that you hear and the books that you read. Indeed, the image of the Dying Gladiator forms a part of the mental furnishing of every highly-cultivated intellect in the civilized world."

CHAPTER VIII

THE TARPEIAN ROCK

One morning while Mr. George and Rollo were taking breakfast together in the dining room of the hotel, Mr. George remarked that he had received some news that morning.

"Is it good news, or bad news?" asked Rollo.

"It is good for me," replied Mr. George, "but I rather think you will consider it bad for you."

"Tell me what it is," said Rollo, "and then I will tell you how I consider it."

So Mr. George informed Rollo that the news which he had received was, that there had been an arrival from America, and that the last night's post had brought the papers to town.

"And so," said Mr. George, "I am going to spend the morning at Piale's[6] library, reading the papers, and you will be left to entertain yourself."

[Footnote 6: Pronounced *Pe-ah-ly's*.]

"O, that's no matter," said Rollo. "I can get Charles Beekman to go with me. We can take care of ourselves very well."

"What will you do?" asked Mr. George.

"I want to go and see the Tarpeian Rock," said Rollo. "I read about that rock, and about Tarpeia, in a history in America, and I want to see how the rock looks."

"Do you know where it is?" asked Mr. George.

"No," said Rollo; "but I can find out."

"Very well," said Mr. George; "then I leave you to take care of yourself. You can get Charles to go, if his mother will trust him with you."

"She will, I am sure," said Rollo.

"Why, you got lost when you took him the other day," said Mr. George, "and you had ever so much difficulty in finding your way home again."

"O, no, uncle George," said Rollo, "we did not have any difficulty at all. We only had a little fun."

Soon after breakfast Mr. George bade Rollo good by, and went off to the bookstore and library, where he was to see and read the American papers. As soon as his uncle had gone, Rollo went up to Mrs. Beekman's room, and knocked at the door. A well-dressed man servant came to the door. It was Mr. Beekman's courier.

"Walk in, Mr. Rollo," said the courier; "Mrs. Beekman and Charles will come in a minute."

So Rollo went in. The room was a small parlor, very beautifully furnished. In a few minutes Mrs. Beekman and Charles came in, followed by Charles's sister, a lively young lady about twelve years of age. Her name was Almira, though they usually called her Allie.

Rollo informed Mrs. Beekman, when she came into the room, that he had come to ask her to allow Charles to go and make an excursion with him. He was going, he said, to see the Tarpeian Rock.

"O, I would not go to see the Tarpeian Rock," said Mrs. Beekman. "Some ladies of my acquaintance went to see it the other day, and they said it was nothing at all."

"Ah, yes, mother!" said Charles, in an entreating tone of voice, "let me go with Rollo."

"Why, there is nothing at all to see," said Mrs. Beekman. "It is only a small, steep face of a rock in a bank. On the Hudson River Railroad you see rocks and precipices forty times as picturesque, all along the way."

Still Rollo and Charles were very desirous to go. The truth was, it was not so much what they expected to see at the end of the excursion, which made it so alluring to them, as the interest and excitement of the various adventures which they thought they would meet with on the way. Finally Mrs. Beekman said that she had not the least objection in the world to their going to see the rock, only she was herself perfectly convinced that they would not find any thing worth seeing.

"I wish Allie could go too," said Rollo.

"Yes, mother," said Allie, clapping her hands.

"Why, do you care about seeing the Tarpeian Rock?" asked her mother.

"Yes, mother," said Allie, "I wish to see it very much, though I don t know what it is. What is it, Rollo?"

"I'll tell you all about it on the way," said Rollo, "if you can only go with us."

"But she cannot walk there," said Mrs. Beekman. "No lady ever walks in Rome."

"I will take a carriage," said Rollo.

"I am afraid you don't know how to manage about a carriage," said Mrs. Beekman.

"Yes, mother," replied Charles, "he knows how to manage about a carriage perfectly well. I tried him the other day."

Mrs. Beekman finally gave a tardy and reluctant consent to the children's proposal. She did not manage the case very wisely. She should have considered in the first instance what her decision ought to be, and then she should have adhered to it. If she was going to consent at all, she should have consented cordially, and at once. For parents first to refuse their children's request, and then allow themselves to be induced to change their determination by the entreaties and persuasions of the children themselves, is bad management.

Allie went into her mother's bed room to get ready, and in a few minutes returned, her countenance beaming with animation and pleasure.

They all went down to the door of the hotel. There were

several carriages standing in the square. The coachmen, as soon as they saw the party at the door, all began to hold up their whips, and to call to Rollo. Some of them began to move their horses towards him.

Rollo glanced his eyes rapidly at the several coaches, and selecting the one which he thought looked the best, he beckoned to the coachman of it. The coachman immediately drew up to the door. He then jumped down from the box, and opened the carriage door.

Before getting in, however, Rollo wished to make his bargain; so he said to the coachman,—

"To the Capitol. Two pauls."

He spoke these words in the Italian language. He had learned the Italian for "two pauls" long before, and he had looked out the Italian name for the Capitol in his Guide Book that morning, so as to be all ready. The Italian name which he found was *Campidoglio*.

The coachman hesitated a moment, and then said, holding up three fingers at the same time,—

"Three pauls."

Of course he spoke in Italian.

Rollo, instead of answering him, immediately began to turn away and look out towards the other carriages.

"*Si, signore, si,*" said the coachman. "Two pauls let it be."

So he held open the carriage door wider than ever, and Rollo assisted Allie to get in. He and Charles followed, and then the coachman drove away.

"You agreed to give him too much," said Charles, as soon as they were seated. "A paul and a half is the regular fare."

"I know it," said Rollo; "but I always offer a little more than the regular fare, especially when I have a lady with me, for then they have not a word to say."

"But this man had a word to say," replied Charles. "He wanted you to give him three pauls."

"Yes," said Rollo, "sometimes they try a little to make a dispute; but they have no chance at all, and they give right up."

Rollo had ordered the coachman to drive to the Capitol, because he had found, by studying the map and the Guide Book, that the entrance to the enclosure where the Tarpeian Rock was to be seen was very near there. He had examined the map attentively, and so he knew exactly which way he must go after being set down at the foot of the Capitol stairs.

Accordingly, when the carriage stopped, Rollo got out first himself, and then helped Allie and Charles out. He paid the coachman the price agreed upon, and a couple of coppers over for *buono mano*.

"Now," said he to Charles and Allie, "follow me."

Rollo went on a little way along a winding street, and then turning to the right, began to go up a steep ascent, formed of very broad steps, which seemed to lead to a higher street. As soon as the party began to go up these steps, they saw several children running down from above to meet them. When these children reached the place where Rollo was, they began saying something very eagerly in Italian, scrambling up the steps again at the same time, so as to keep up with Rollo and his party.

"What do these children want?" asked Allie.

"I don't know," said Rollo. "I have not the least idea."

"I suppose they are begging," said Charles.

"No," said Allie. "If they were begging, they would hold out their hands."

At the top of the stairs Rollo and his party were met by half a dozen more children, so that there were now eight or ten in all. They ran on before and by the side of Rollo and his party, all looking very eager and animated, talking incessantly, and beckoning and pointing forward.

"Ah!" said Rollo, "I know. They want to show us the way to the Tarpeian Rock."

"But you said you knew the way," said Allie.

"I said I could find it," replied Rollo, "and so I can; but I am willing to pay one of these children for showing me, but not all. Stop a minute, till I choose. Or, rather, you may choose, Allie," he added.

The party now stopped, while Allie surveyed the ragged and wretched-looking group before her.

"There is not a pretty child among them," said Allie.

"You should not look for the best looking one, Allie," said Charles. "You should choose the *worst* looking one. She is likely to need it most. Pretty looking girls get along well enough."

"Then I choose that poor barefooted girl, that looks so pale," said Allie.

"Yes," said Rollo; "she looks as if she had had a fever."

So Rollo pointed to the girl, and showed her a copper, which he took for the purpose from his pocket. At the same time he made a waving motion with his hand to the rest, to denote that he did not wish for their services, and that they might go away.

The barefooted girl seemed greatly pleased. Her pale and emaciated face was lighted up with a smile of pleasure. She ran along forward, beckoning to Rollo and his party to follow.

The rest of the children, though they understood perfectly the signal of dismission that Rollo had made to them, were determined not to be sent off in that way; so they went on gesticulating and clamoring as much as ever.

Rollo paid no attention to them, but walked on with Charles and Allie at his side. Presently their guide, and all the other children with her, stopped at a sort of gateway in a wall. By the side of the gateway there was an iron ring hanging by a chain. Two or three of the children seized this ring together and pulled it, by which means a bell was rung inside. The other children crowded together on each side of this gate, leaving room, however, for Rollo and his party to go through, and all held out their hands for money.

"I am only going to pay the one that I engaged," said Rollo; "but, poor thing, I mean to give her two coppers, instead of one, she looks so sick and miserable."

"So I would," said Allie. "And here," she added, putting her hand into her pocket and taking out a Roman copper coin, "I have got a penny here; you may give her that, too."

"That is not a penny," said Charles. "That is a *baioccho*."

"Never mind," said Allie; "*I* call it a penny. I can't remember the other name. Besides, it is all the same thing."

Rollo gave the three pieces of money to the poor girl, and the rest of the children, when they saw how generous he was, became more clamorous than ever. But Rollo paid no heed to them. Indeed, a moment after he had paid his little guide her money, the gate opened, and the party went in. The poor children were all left outside, and shut out.

It was a small girl, about thirteen years old, that opened the gate.

Rollo and his party found themselves ushered into a sort of garden. The girl led the way along a narrow path between beds of beans, lettuce, and other garden vegetables. Besides these vegetables, there were groups of shrubbery here and there, among which roses and other flowers were blooming. This garden seemed to be in the heart of the city, for it was bordered on three sides by buildings, and on the fourth by a low wall, which appeared to be built on the brow of a hill, for the roofs and chimneys of other houses, situated on a lower level, could be seen over it below.

The girl led the way to a place by this wall, where, by looking over, there could be seen, at a distance along the hill, a small place where the rock which formed the face of it was precipitous. The precipice seemed to be about ten or fifteen feet high.

"Is that the Tarpeian Rock?" asked Rollo.

The girl who conducted them did not reply, not knowing any language but the Italian.

"I've seen a great deal prettier rocks in America," said Allie.

"Then are you sorry you came?" asked Rollo.

"O, no!" said Allie; "I am very glad I came. But what is it that makes this rock so famous?"

"Why, it is the place where, in old times, a very remarkable thing happened," replied Rollo. "I read the story in the history of Rome, when I was studying history in America. There was a girl named Tarpeia. She lived somewhere near the top of this rock, and the wall of the city came somewhere along here, and there was a gate. The Sabines made war against the Romans, and came to attack the city, but they could not get in on account of the walls. One day Tarpeia was on the wall looking down, and she saw some of the Sabine soldiers walking about below."

"Why did not they shoot her?" asked Charles.

"O, they had no motive for shooting her," replied Rollo.

"She was a nice, pretty girl, I suppose, and they liked to look at her, and to talk with her. Besides, they had a cunning plan in view. They asked her whether they could not induce her to open the gates and let them into the city. She said she would do it if they would give her what they wore on their arms. She meant their bracelets. The soldiers in those days used to adorn themselves with rings, and bracelets, and other such things. But then, besides these bracelets they wore their shields and bucklers on their arms. These were very heavy things, made of iron, and covered with hides. So they agreed that they would give her what they wore on their arms, secretly meaning that they would throw their bucklers upon her; but she thought they meant that they would give her their bracelets.

"So that night," continued Rollo, "the soldiers came, bringing a great many other soldiers with them, and Tarpeia opened the gate and let them in. The whole troop rushed by her into the town, as fast as they could go, and as they passed they all threw their bucklers upon poor Tarpeia, till she was crushed to death, and buried up by them. It was pretty near this rock where this happened, and so, forever after, they called it the Tarpeian Rock, and that is the reason why so many people come to see it."

There was a moment's pause after Rollo had finished his story, during which Allie looked quite concerned. At length she said, in a very earnest tone,—

"I think it was a shame!"

"I think they served her just right," said Charles.

"O, Charles!" replied Alice, "how can you say so?"

The girl who had conducted the party through the garden now began to lead the way back again, and they all followed her. As she walked along, the girl began to gather flowers from the beds and borders, and finally made quite a pretty bouquet. When she got to the gate, and was ready to open it, she presented this bouquet in a very polite and graceful manner to Allie. Rollo took some money from his pocket, and put it into her hand; and then she opened the gate, and let them all out.

"How much did you pay her, Rollo?" asked Charles.

"I paid her double," said Rollo, "because she was so polite as to give Allie such a pretty bouquet."

Allie was now more pleased with her bouquet than before. It pleased her extremely to find that Rollo took so much interest in her receiving a bouquet as to pay something specially for it.

So they all went down the steps which led to the foot of the Capitol Hill.

"Shall we walk home?" asked Rollo, "or shall I find a carriage, so that we can ride?"

"Let us walk," replied Allie, "and then we shall be longer on the way."

Just then Rollo, looking at the sky, saw that there were some rather threatening clouds diffused over it. Indeed, on putting out his hand, he plainly felt a sprinkling of rain.

"It is going to rain," said he, "and so we shall be obliged to ride. But we can make it longer by stopping to see something on the way."

"Well," said Allie, "let's do it. What shall we stop to see?"

"If there is going to be a shower," said Rollo, "it would be a good time to stop and see the Pantheon."

"What is the Pantheon?" asked Allie.

"It is an immense round church, with a great hole in the roof," replied Rollo.

"Why don't they mend the hole?" asked Charles.

"O, they made it so on purpose," said Rollo.

"Made it on purpose!" repeated Allie. "I never heard of such a thing. I should think the rain would come in."

"It does come in," said Rollo, "and that is the reason why I want to go and see the Pantheon in the time of a shower. It is so curious to see the rain falling down slowly to the pavement. You see, the church is round, and there is a dome over it, and in the centre of the dome they left a great round hole."

"How big?" asked Allie.

"It is twenty-eight feet across," said Rollo; "but you would not think it so big when you come to see it. It is up so high that it looks very small. We know how big it is by the size of the wet spot on the floor."

By the time that the party had arrived at this point in the conversation, Rollo saw a carriage standing in the street at a little distance before him, and he made a signal to the coachman to come to him. The coachman came. Rollo made his bargain with him, and they all got in. The coachman drove immediately to the Pantheon, and they arrived there just as the shower began to come on.

Before the church was an immense portico, supported by columns. The columns, and the whole entablature which they supported, were darkened by time, and cracked, and chipped, and broken in the most remarkable manner. Allie and Charles stood under the portico and looked around, while Rollo paid the coachman.

There was a large open square before the Pantheon, with an ancient and very remarkable looking fountain in the centre of it. There was a basin around this fountain, into which monstrous mouths, carved in marble, were spouting water. When Rollo had paid the coachman, he led the way into the church. Allie and Charles followed him. They found themselves ushered into an immense circular interior, with rows of columns all around the sides, and chapels, and sculptures, and paintings, and beautiful panels of variegated marbles between them.

Overhead was an immense dome. This dome is nearly a hundred and fifty feet high, and the circular opening in the centre of it is about thirty feet across. Through this opening the rain was descending in a steady but gentle shower. It was very curious to look up and see the innumerable drops falling slowly from the bright opening above, down to the marble floor. This opening is the only window. There is no other place, as you will see by the engraving, where light can come in.

The margin of the opening is formed of an immense brass ring. Such a ring is necessary in a structure like this, and it must be of great thickness and strength, to resist the pressure of the stones crowding in upon it all around.

This Pantheon was built by the ancient Romans, two thousand years ago. What it was built for originally nobody now knows. In modern times it has been changed into a church. It is immensely large, being nearly a hundred and fifty feet in diameter, and a hundred and fifty feet high. If you will inquire and ascertain what is the size of some large building in your vicinity, and compare it with these dimensions, you will form a clearer idea of the magnitude of this ancient edifice than you can acquire in any other way.

Rollo and his party rambled about the Pantheon, looking at the statues, and paintings, and chapels, and observing the groups of pilgrims and of visitors that were continually coming and going, for nearly an hour. By this time the shower had entirely passed away, and the sun having come out bright, they all walked home.

Jacob Abbott

CHAPTER IX

GOING TO OSTIA

While Rollo was at Rome, he made the acquaintance of a boy named Copley. Copley was an English boy, and he was about a year older than Rollo. Rollo first saw him at the door of the hotel, as he, Copley, was dismounting from his horse, on his return from a ride which he had been taking into the country. He had been attended on his ride by a servant man named Thomas. Thomas dismounted from his horse first, and held the bridle of Copley's horse while Copley dismounted.

"There!" said Copley, walking off with a very grand air, and leaving his horse in Thomas's hands; "take the horse, Thomas, and never bring me such an animal as that again. Next time I ride I shall take Jessie."

"But Mr. William has forbidden me to give you Jessie," said Thomas. "He says she is not safe."

"It's none of his business," said Copley. "He thinks, because he is a little older than I am, and because he is married,—though he has not been married much more than a month,—that he has a right to order me about just as he pleases. And I am determined not to submit to it—

would you?"

These last words were addressed to Rollo. Copley had been advancing towards the door of the hotel, while he had been speaking, and had now just reached the step where Rollo was standing.

"Who is he?" asked Rollo. "Who is William?"

"He is my brother," said Copley; "but that has nothing to do with it."

"Are you under his care?" asked Rollo.

"Why, I am travelling with him," said Copley; "but he has no business on that account to lord it over me. I have as good a right to have my way as he has to have his."

Some further conversation then followed between Copley and Rollo, in which the former said that he had been for several weeks in Rome, in company with his brother. He had an uncle, too, in town, he said, at another hotel.

"But I stay with my brother," said Copley, "because he is going to make a longer journey, and I want to go with him."

"Where is he going?" asked Rollo.

"Why, we have engaged a vetturino," replied Copley, "and are going to travel slowly to Florence, and from Florence into the northern part of Italy, to Milan and Venice, and all those places. Then, afterwards, we shall go over, by some of the passes of the Alps, into Switzerland. I like to travel in that way, I have so much fun in seeing the towns and the country. Besides, when we travel with a vetturino, I almost always ride on the outside seat with him, and he lets me drive sometimes."

"Then your uncle is not going that way?" said Rollo.

"No," replied Copley; "he is going directly home by water. He is going down to Civita Vecchia, to take the steamer there for Marseilles, and I don't want to go that way."

Copley then asked Rollo to go out into the Corso with him. He said that he saw a shop there, as he was coming home, which had a great display of whips at the window, and he wanted to buy a whip, so that when they set out on their journey he could have a whip of his own.

"The vetturino never will let me have *his* whip," said he. "The lash is so long that he says I shall get it entangled in the harness. That's no reason, for he is always getting it entangled himself. But that's his excuse, and so I am going to have a whip of my own."

"Well," said Rollo, "I rather think I will go with you; but you must wait here for me a minute or two. I must go up to my room first; but I will come directly down again."

Rollo wished to go up to his room to ask his uncle's permission to go with Copley. He made it an invariable rule never to go any where without his uncle's permission. Mr. George was always ready to give permission in such cases, unless there was some really good and substantial reason for withholding it. And whenever Mr. George withheld his consent from any of Rollo's proposals, Rollo always submitted at once, without making any difficulty, even when he thought that his uncle was wrong, and that he might have consented as well as not.

It was not altogether principle on the part of Rollo, that made him pursue this course; it was in a great measure policy.

"I like travelling about the world with uncle George," he used to say to himself, "and in order that I may travel with him a great deal, I must make it for his interest to take me. That is, I must manage so that he will have a better time when I am with him, than when he goes alone; and in order to do this, I must take care never to give him any trouble or concern of any kind on my account. I must comply with his wishes in every thing, and be satisfied with such pleasures and enjoyments as he fully approves."

Rollo did not think of this altogether of himself. It was his father that put the idea into his mind. He did it in a conversation that he had with Rollo the day before he set out on the journey.

"Rollo, my boy," said he, "in going on this journey into Italy with your uncle George, there is one danger that you will have to look out for very carefully."

"Getting robbed by the brigands?" asked Rollo.

"No," said Mr. Holiday; "it is something very different from that, and a great deal worse. That is to say, the evil that you have to fear from it is a great deal worse than any thing that would probably happen to you by being robbed. The danger is of your having too much independence, or, rather, a wrong kind of independence. What is independence?"

Rollo reflected a moment in order properly to frame his answer to his father's question. He thought he knew very well what the meaning of the word *independence* was, but he did not readily know how to clothe the meaning in language. At last he said that he thought independence was doing what you thought was best yourself, without regard to what other people thought.

"Very well," said his father. "That's a pretty good definition of it. And now, do you think it is a good quality, or a bad quality?"

"A good quality," said Rollo; "that is, I suppose it is good," he added, hesitatingly, "but I don't know."

"It depends upon circumstances," said Mr. Holiday. "Should you think that firing his gun when *he* thought best, instead of when the *captain* thought best, was a good thing in a soldier, on the field of battle?"

"No, sir," said Rollo.

"And so, would the independence of the colonel of a regiment," continued Mr. Holiday, "in marching when he thought best, instead of when the general ordered him, be a good quality or a bad quality?"

"Bad," said Rollo; "very bad indeed."

"Independence is an excellent quality in its own right and proper sphere," said Mr. Holiday; "but when it takes the form of disregarding or rebelling against right and proper authority, it is a very bad quality. It cannot be tolerated. If it were allowed generally to prevail among mankind, the whole world would be thrown into confusion, and nothing could go on. This is now the kind of independence that you must guard against. You are growing up rapidly, and increasing in strength and knowledge every day. You are becoming a young man, and in a great many of the situations in which you are placed, you are fully competent to take care of yourself. Still you are what the law calls a minor. That is, you have not arrived at an age when you can safely be your own master, and support and take care of yourself. Consequently, the law makes it your father's duty, for some years to come, to furnish money for your support, and to provide for you all necessary protection. And the same law makes it your duty to be under my direction, to conform your conduct to my judgment; or, in other words, to do, not as *you* think best, but as I, or whomsoever I may delegate to act in my stead, thinks best. This is reasonable. As long as a boy depends upon his father for the means of his support, it is right that he should act as his father's judgment dictates. It will be time enough for him to expect that he should act according to his own judgment, in his conduct, when he is able to earn his own living, and so release his father from all responsibility on his account. In a word, the pecuniary responsibility of the father, and the moral obligation of the son, go together."

"Yes, father," said Rollo; "I think that is all true."

"And now," continued Mr. Holiday, "I put you, for this journey, under your uncle George's care. I delegate my parental power over you to him. It is your duty, therefore, to obey him in all things, and to comply with all his wishes, just as you would if I were in his place."

"Yes, father," said Rollo, "I will."

"Besides being your duty," added Mr. Holiday, "it is greatly for your interest to do so. If you begin to show your independence, as it is sometimes called, and insist on doing what you think is best, instead of what he thinks is best, so as to cause him trouble, and make him feel

Jacob Abbott

anxious and uneasy on your account, you will spoil the pleasure of his journey, and he will not wish to take you with him again."

Mr. Holiday had some further conversation with Rollo on the subject, and the effect of what he said was to lead Rollo to think more than he otherwise would have done on the proper course which a boy ought to pursue when travelling under the charge of his uncle, and he resolved that he would, in all cases, not only obey implicitly his uncle's commands, but that he would comply readily and cordially with his wishes, whenever he could ascertain them.

Accordingly, in this case, he would not go even out into the Corso without first going up to obtain his uncle's permission. He opened the door of the room, and found his uncle there, writing a letter.

"Uncle George," said he, "here is a boy down below, who asks me to go out into the Corso with him."

"What boy is it?" asked Mr. George.

"I don't know what his name is," said Rollo. "He is an English boy, I suppose. He just came in from taking a ride on horseback."

"How long shall you probably be gone?" said Mr. George.

"I don't know," said Rollo, hesitating. "Perhaps about half an hour."

"Very well,' said Mr. George; "you can be gone two hours if you choose. If you form any plan that will require more time than that, come home first and let me know."

So Rollo went down stairs again, and having joined Copley at the door, they went together out towards the Corso.

In the mean time, Copley's brother William and his wife were waiting in their room for Copley to come up. They knew at what hour he would return from his ride, and they had formed a plan for going in a carriage out upon the Appian Way, to see some ancient ruins there. They knew very well that Copley would not care any thing about the ruins, but he always liked to go with them when they took drives in the environs of Rome. The special reason why Copley was so much interested in going on these excursions was, that he was accustomed, in such cases, to sit on the front seat with the coachman, as he did when travelling with the vetturins, and sometimes he obtained permission to drive a little, by secretly offering the coachman a piece of money. Mr. William had charged his brother to come up to the parlor as soon as he came home from his ride, and Copley ought to have done so. But it was never Copley's practice to pay much heed to requests of this kind from his brother.

Mr. William, having waited for some time after he had seen the two horses arrive at the door, wondering all the time why Copley did not come up, went down to the door to inquire what had become of him. The concierge informed him that Copley had gone away with another boy, out to the Corso. So Mr. William ordered the carriage, and he and his wife went away on their excursion alone.

Rollo and Copley had a very pleasant walk along the Corso. They were obliged, however, to walk in the middle of the street, for the sidewalks were so narrow and so irregular in shape, sometimes growing narrower and narrower, until at length there was scarcely any thing but the curb-stone left, that Rollo and Copley could not walk upon them.

At last, however, they came to the place where Copley had seen the whips. Copley had plenty of money, but I do not know how he would have managed to buy one of the whips, if Rollo had not been with him; for the man who had them to sell could only speak French and Italian, and Copley did not know either of these languages. He had been studying French, it is true, for several years in school, but he had taken no interest in learning the language, and the little knowledge of it which he had acquired was not of such a character as to be of any use to him. As to the Italian, he knew nothing at all of it.

Accordingly, Rollo acted as interpreter.

"I might have brought our courier with us," said Copley, "only it is such a bore to have him about; and you do just as well."

After having bought the whip, Copley proposed that they should go to the diligence office and see if there were any diligences there about setting out on their journeys. The diligence office which Copley referred to was not in the Corso, but in another street, at right angles to it. When the boys reached the office, they found that there were no diligences there; so they rambled on without much idea of where they were going, until at length they came to the river, near one of the bridges leading across it. A short distance below the bridge, there was a small steamboat coming up the river.

"Ah, look there!" said Copley. "There's a steamer coming! Where do you suppose that steamer is coming from?"

"It is coming from Ostia, I suppose," said Rollo. "At any rate, I know that there is a steamer that goes to Ostia."

"Let us go there," said Copley. "Where is Ostia?"

"It is at the mouth of the river," said Rollo. "You may know that from the name. *Ostia* is the Latin word for *mouth*."

"I hate Latin," said Copley.

The little steamer came rounding up to a pier not far below the bridge. Copley and Rollo leaned over the parapet, and looked to see the passengers get out; but there were very few passengers to come. The boys then went down towards the pier, and on inquiring of a gentleman whom they saw there, they found that the boat went down the river to Ostia every morning, and returned every night, and Copley immediately conceived the idea of going down in her.

"Let's go down to-morrow," said he. "It is just far enough for a pleasant sail."

Rollo's imagination was quite taken with the idea of sailing down to Ostia. There seems to be something specially attractive to boys in the idea of sailing down to the mouths of rivers. It is so pleasant to watch the gradual widening of the stream, and to meet vessels coming up, and to see the fishermen's boats, and the nets spread on the land, and the little inlets, with the tide flowing in and out, and other indications of the approach towards the sea. Besides, Rollo wished very much to see what sort of a place Ostia was.

However, he would not positively promise to go. He said

he should like to go very much, but that he could not decide the question until he should go home.

"I must see uncle George first," said Rollo. "It is possible that he may have formed some engagement for me to-morrow."

"O, never mind what engagement he has formed," said Copley. "Tell him that you can't go with him, because you have agreed to go down the river with me."

"No," said Rollo, shaking his head.

"Why, what a little fool you are!" said Copley.

After remaining some time on the bridge, looking at the steamer, the boys returned home. Rollo took care to arrive at the hotel before the two hours were expired. Mr. George had just finished his letter, and was folding it up and sealing it.

"Well, Rollo," said Mr. George, "have you had a pleasant walk?"

"Very pleasant, indeed," said Rollo. "We walked in the Corso till Copley had bought his whip, and then we went on till we came to the bridge, and there we saw a steamboat which goes to Ostia and back. Copley wants me to go down with him in her to-morrow. We shall get back about this time, I suppose."

Mr. George was at this time just writing the address on the back of his letter. He did not say any thing, but Rollo observed a very slight and almost imperceptible shaking of his head.

"You don't like the plan very well, uncle George," said Rollo.

"Not very well," said Mr. George. "I feel a little afraid of it."

"Then it is of no consequence," said Rollo. "I don't care a great deal about going."

Most boys, perhaps, under these circumstances, would have asked why, in order that, after hearing their uncle's objections to their plans, they might argue against them. But Rollo knew very well that this would be very bad policy for him.

"If uncle George finds that he has a long argument to maintain against me, every time that he refuses me any thing," said he to himself, "he will soon get tired of having me under his care."

So he acquiesced at once in what he perceived was his uncle's opinion, and resolved to tell Copley, when he saw him, that he could not go to Ostia.

Copley was to have called that evening at Rollo's room, to obtain his answer; but on further reflection, he concluded not to do so.

Indeed, he had a secret feeling that neither Rollo's uncle nor his own brother would approve of the plan of two such boys going alone, in such a country, on an expedition which was entirely outside of the usual range of tourists and travellers. That this expedition *was* outside the range was evident from the character of the steamboat that the boys had seen, which was evidently not intended for the conveyance of ladies and gentlemen, but of people of the country—and those, moreover, of the lowest class.

So Copley concluded that if he were to go at all to Ostia, it would be necessary for him to go by stealth, and he resolved not to say any thing about his plan to his brother or sister. He was very sure, too, that Rollo would fail of obtaining his uncle's consent. So he concluded to say no more to Rollo on the subject, but instead of that, he proposed the plan to another boy of his acquaintance, who lodged with his friends at another hotel.

"The best way will be," said he, when he made the proposal, "for us not to tell any body where we are going."

"Then they'll wonder where we are," said the boy, "and be frightened half to death about us."

"But we can leave word when we go, with the porter of the hotel, or the concierge," said Copley, "that we have gone down the river in the steamboat, and shall not be back till night."

"Good," said the other boy; "that's what we'll do."

Accordingly, the next morning, the two boys left word at their respective hotels where they were going, and set forth. They stole away very secretly, and after running round the corner, they crept along close to the wall of the hotel, until they thought they were at a safe distance. They reached the boat in good season, went on board, and in due time set sail.

About ten o'clock, when the two boys had been gone about an hour, Mr. William began to miss his brother, and to wonder where he had gone. So he rang the bell, and his courier came into the room.

"Pacifico," said Mr. William, "do you know where Copley is?"

"No, sir," said Pacifico; "I did not see him from since it was nine o'clock."

"Go down below," said Mr. William, "and inquire of the concierge and the porters if they have seen him, or know where he is."

Mr. William followed Pacifico as he went out, in order to speak a moment to a friend of his who occupied the next apartment. As he came back he met Pacifico at the head of the stairs, and received his answer there. The answer was, that Copley had gone down the river to Ostia with another boy.

Mr. William was greatly astonished to hear this. He, however, said nothing to Pacifico, but after pausing a moment, as if reflecting upon what he had heard, he went back into his own apartment.

"Maria," said he, addressing his young wife, "where do you think Copley has gone?"

"I cannot imagine," said Maria.

"He has gone down the Tiber in the steamer to Ostia," replied Mr. William.

"Is it possible?" exclaimed Maria, in astonishment.

"Yes," said William; "and I am very glad of it."

"Glad of it?" repeated Maria, surprised more and more.

"Yes," said Mr. William; "for it decides me what to do. I shall send him home with his uncle. I have been half inclined to do this for some time, and this settles the question. It destroys all the peace and comfort of our journey to have a boy with us that is determined to have his own way, without regard to the inconvenience or anxiety that he occasions me."

"But how will you manage to get him to go with his uncle?" said Maria. "He will refuse to go, and insist on accompanying us, for his uncle is going directly home, which is what he does not wish to do."

"I'll manage that," said Mr. William. "I'll take a hint from his own way of proceeding. I will go off and leave him."

"O husband," said Maria, "that will never do."

"You'll see how I will manage it," said Mr. William.

So saying, Mr. William rang the bell. Pacifico immediately appeared.

"I wish to write a letter," said Mr. William. "Bring me some paper, and pen and ink."

Pacifico brought the writing materials, and laid them on the table.

"I have concluded to leave town this afternoon," said Mr. William, as he took up the pen and began to make preparations to write. "I intend to go as far as Civita Castellana to-night. We will set out at two o'clock. I wish you to go and find our vetturino, and direct him to be here half an hour before that time with the carriage, to load the baggage. He knows that we were going soon, and he will be prepared. In the mean time you may get our baggage ready. Copley's trunk, however, is not to go. Pack that, and send it by a porter over to the Hotel d'Amerique. I am going to leave him there under the care of his uncle."

"Very well, sir," said Pacifico; "I shall do it."

Pacifico retired, and Mr. William proceeded to write his letter. When it was finished, he read it to his wife, as follows. It was addressed to his father in England.

"ROME, June 20, 1858.

"DEAR FATHER: We are all well, and, on the whole, have enjoyed our residence in Rome very much. We are now, however, about ready to leave. We set off this afternoon for Florence and the north of Italy.

"I have concluded, all things considered, to let Copley return to you with his uncle. Though a pretty good boy in other respects, he does not seem to be quite willing enough to submit to my direction, to make it pleasant for me, or safe for him, that we should travel together. I will not say that it is his *fault* altogether. It is perhaps because there is not difference enough in our ages for him to feel that I ought to have any authority over him. At any rate, he is unwilling to acknowledge my authority, and he takes so many liberties that I am kept in a constant state of anxiety on his account. Besides, I do not think that it is safe for him to be so much at his own disposal. This country is full of thieves, brigands, and rogues, of the most desperate and reckless character; and young men sometimes suffer extremely in falling into their hands. Copley is not aware of the danger, and he thinks that the restraints which I feel compelled to impose upon him are unnecessary and vexatious. Often he will not submit to them. To-day, he has gone down the river on board one of the country steamers, without saying any thing to me about it; and, though I do not suppose he will get into any difficulty, in making such an excursion, still the fact that he takes the liberty of doing such things keeps me continually uneasy about him, and there is danger that, sooner or later, he will get into some serious trouble.

"I have, accordingly, concluded to leave him under uncle's charge, with a view of having him return with uncle to England, by way of the Mediterranean. Uncle will leave here in a few days, and you may accordingly expect to see Copley at home again in the course of a week after receiving this.

"With love from Maria and myself for all at home, I am your dutiful son,

"WILLIAM GRANT."

Mr. William sealed his letter, and then took it down to the "bureau," as the hotel office is called, where he left it with the secretary of the hotel, to be sent to the post office.

He then went out at the front door of the hotel to the public square before it, and there taking a carriage, he ordered the coachman to drive to the Hotel d'Amerique. When arrived there, he went to his uncle's apartment, and explained the plan which he had formed, and the reason for it. His uncle said that he would very readily take Copley under his charge. Mr. William then said that he was intending to leave town that day, but he should leave Thomas at his hotel to wait for Copley, and bring him over to the Hotel d'Amerique as soon as he returned.

This arrangement was carried into effect. Mr. William directed Thomas to remain in town, to take care of Copley on his return from Ostia, and deliver him safely into his uncle's hands. It occasioned Mr. William no inconvenience to leave Thomas behind for a day, since, though Thomas usually travelled in the same carriage with the family, the vetturino himself always drove. Thomas, together with Pacifico, the courier, rode on an outside seat in front, while Copley sometimes rode inside, though more frequently on the driver's seat, by the side of the vetturino.

"Thomas," said Mr. Grant, in giving Thomas his instructions, "I am going to set out on my journey this afternoon, but I shall leave you behind, to come on to-night by the diligence. You will find me at the Hotel of the Post, at Civita Castellana. I wish you to wait here until Copley comes home, and then tell him that I have gone out of town, and shall not be back to-night, and that he is going to spend the night at the Hotel d'Amerique with his uncle. Do not tell him where I have gone, nor that you are coming after me. His uncle will tell him all to-morrow morning."

In the mean time, while these occurrences had been taking place at the hotel, Copley and his companion had been sailing down the river on board the little steamboat. They had, on the whole, a pretty pleasant time, though they were somewhat disappointed in the scenery on the banks of the river. The country was perfectly bare of trees, and destitute of all cultivation. There were no villages, and scarcely a human habitation to be seen. The boys, however, met with no trouble, and returned safely home about four o'clock.

Copley found Thomas waiting for him at the hotel door.

"Mr. Copley." said Thomas, as Copley advanced towards the door, "your brother has gone out of town, and will not be back to-night, and I was to wait here for you, and tell you that you were to go and spend the night at your uncle's apartment at the Hotel d'Amerique."

"Good!" said Copley. He felt quite relieved to find that his brother had gone away, as he thus escaped the danger of being called to account for his misdemeanor.

"Where has he gone?" asked Copley.

"I can't say,' said Thomas; "but perhaps your uncle can tell you."

By the phrase "I can't say," Thomas secretly meant that he was not at liberty to say, though Copley understood him to mean that he did not know.

"Very well," said Copley; "I don't care where he has gone. It makes no difference to me."

Copley found that it did make some difference to him, when he learned, the next morning, that his brother had set out on his journey to the north of Italy, and to Switzerland, and had left him behind to return home at once with his uncle by sea. His uncle did not tell him that night where his brother had gone, for fear that Copley might make some difficulty, by insisting on going on after him in the diligence with Thomas. Accordingly, when Copley asked the question, his uncle only answered vaguely, that his brother had gone out somewhere into the environs of Rome. The next morning, however, he handed Copley a note which his brother had left for him, which note Copley, on opening it, found to be as follows:—

"WEDNESDAY MORNING.

"DEAR COPLEY: I have concluded to set out this afternoon on my journey north. I am sorry that you are not here to bid me good by. I did not know that you were going down the river.

"It must be hard for a boy as old as you to be under the command of one who is, after all, only his brother,— and not a great many years older than he is himself,— for I am not quite ten years older than you. I know you have found this hard, and so I have concluded that you had better return home with uncle. One of these days, when you grow up to manhood, you can make a journey into Italy again, and then you will be your own master, and can do as you please, without any danger. Wishing you a very pleasant voyage,

"I am your affectionate brother,

"WILLIAM GRANT."

Copley's indignation and rage at reading this letter seemed at first to know no bounds. He was, however, entirely helpless. His brother had gone, and he did not even know what road he had taken. Thomas had gone, too, so that there was no help for him whatever.

In two days after that, he went with his uncle to Civita Vecchia, the port of Rome, on the Mediterranean, and there embarked on board the steamer "for Marseilles direct," and so returned to England.

CHAPTER X

THE VATICAN

On the day when Rollo went with Charles and Allie to see the Tarpeian Rock, the reader will perhaps recollect that Mr. George was engaged at the reading room in reading the American papers which had that morning arrived. When Rollo returned from his excursion, he found that Mr. George had not got home, and he accordingly concluded to go to the reading room and see if he could find him.

This reading room is attached to an English bookstore and library, and is a great place of resort for visitors at Rome. It is situated at the end of the Piazza di Spagna, which is one of the principal and most frequented public squares in Rome. This square contains several of the chief hotels, and a great many shops. The bookstore of Piale is the general centre of news and intelligence for all English and American visitors. Here people come to make inquiries for their friends, for there is a register kept at the library with the names of all the English and American visitors in Rome recorded in it, and the addresses of the hotels or private houses where they are lodging. Here all sorts of notices are posted up, such as advertisements of things lost or found, of parties forming for excursions, of couriers wanting places or families wanting couriers, of paintings for sale, carriages for sale or for hire,—and all such things.

Piale's establishment contains a number of different rooms. The first that Rollo entered on arriving at the place was the bookstore. This was a small room. There was a desk at one end, where a clerk was sitting. There were shelves filled with books all around the room, and a large table in the centre, which was also covered with books arranged in tiers one above the other in a sloping direction. There were several doors leading off from this apartment, one of which led to a room where a circulating library was kept, and another to the reading room.

When Rollo entered the bookstore, he saw several groups of visitors there. There were two or three ladies looking over the books on the shelves. There was a group of gentlemen standing near the desk, talking together, with a paper in their hands which seemed to contain a list of names. Just as Rollo entered, a carriage drove up to the door, and two ladies dismounted from it and came in. Rollo's attention was first attracted to these two ladies. One of them, on entering, accosted the clerk, and asked to look at the register. The clerk immediately gave the two ladies seats at a side table, where there was a large book full of names and addresses. The ladies sat down, and began to look over the book. They had just arrived from Naples, and they wished to know what friends and acquaintances of theirs there were in town.

Rollo began to examine the books on the table, or counter, in the middle of the room, and while doing so he happened to pass near the gentlemen that were looking at the paper.

"We want twelve," said one of the gentlemen, "and we have got only nine."

"Yes," said the other, "we want three more. It must be that there are a great many in town who would like to go, if we could only find them out."

Rollo's attention was immediately arrested by these words. It was obvious that the gentlemen were forming a party to go somewhere, or to see something, and he felt quite confident that his uncle George would like to join them.

"At any rate," said he to himself, "*I* should like to go, wherever it is."

So Rollo summoned courage to accost the persons who were consulting together, and to ask them if they wished to find some gentlemen to make up a party.

"Gentlemen or ladies either," said one of them, "no matter which. We are making up a party to go and see the statues in the Vatican by torch light."

When Rollo heard the words "torch light," his interest in the proposed party was greatly increased, and he said he had no doubt that his uncle would like to go.

"I am very sure he would like to go," said Rollo, "and to take me."

"Very well," said one of the gentlemen, "that will make two. And we only want three. Where is your uncle?"

"He is in the reading room," said Rollo. "Wait a moment, and I'll call him."

"That's right," said the gentleman. "Tell him it will cost us a scudo and a half apiece."

So Rollo, taking out half a paul from his pocket,—that being the price of admission to the reading room for a single day,—and giving it to the clerk at the desk, opened a door by the side of the desk, and passed into the reading room. Instead of being only one reading room, however, he found that there were two, with an open door leading from one to the other. There were a great number of very comfortable sofas and arm chairs all about these rooms, and great tables in the middle of them covered with newspapers and magazines. The walls of both rooms were completely covered with paintings of all sizes, most of which had been left there for sale. There were a great many gentlemen sitting around the tables and upon the sofas, reading. Among them Rollo soon found Mr. George. He had established himself in a comfortable arm chair, near a great window that looked out upon the square. But he was obliged to keep the curtain down, on account of the beggars outside, that gave him no peace as long as they could see him.

"Uncle George," said Rollo, "here are some gentlemen who want to make up a party to go and see something by torch light, and I thought that perhaps you and I would like to join it."

"Where is it that they are going?" asked Mr. George—"to the Vatican?"

"Yes," said Rollo, "it is the Vatican. A scudo and a half apiece."

"Very well," said Mr. George. "I should like to go. Where are the gentlemen?"

"They are out here in the bookstore. Come out and I will show them to you."

So Mr. George laid down his paper, and followed Rollo out into the bookstore. Rollo led the way to the place where the gentlemen were standing, and then introduced his uncle, in a distinct and audible voice, thus,—

"This is my uncle, gentlemen, Mr. George Holiday."

The gentlemen greeted Mr. Holiday in a very polite manner, and informed him of their plan, and that they wanted three more names to make up the necessary number for a party.

And here I ought to say in explanation, that what is called the "Vatican" is a vast collection of very magnificent and imposing buildings,—consisting of palaces, chapels, halls, galleries, and the like, almost without number,— and it is filled with paintings, sculptures, manuscripts, books, jewels, gems, and other curiosities and treasures of incalculable value. It is situated in close proximity to the great Church of St. Peter's—the largest and most gorgeous church in the world. Indeed, the church and the palaces form, as it were, one vast architectural pile, which is of almost inconceivable magnificence and grandeur.

The various edifices which compose the Vatican were several centuries in building, and the immense magnitude and extent of the edifice, and the exhaustless wealth of the treasures of art deposited there, astonish every beholder. The buildings are so extensive that they require eight grand staircases and two hundred smaller ones to gain access to the different stories. There are twenty open courts and over four thousand different rooms. Some of these rooms are galleries nearly a quarter of a mile long, and are filled on each side with sculptures and statuary, or other works of art, from end to end. The length of these galleries is not, however, out of proportion to other parts of the structure. The church of St. Peter's, including the portico, is considerably *more* than a quarter of a mile long.

Now, among the treasures of the Vatican are an immense number of ancient statues which were dug up, in the middle ages, in and around Rome; and some of these sculptures are the most celebrated works of art in the world. They are arranged with great care in a great number of beautiful chambers and halls, and are visited during the daytime by thousands of people that have come to Rome from every part of the world. The picture galleries, the collection of ancient curiosities, and the library rooms containing the books and manuscripts, are also in the same manner thrown open, and they are thronged with visitors almost all the time. These apartments are so numerous and so extensive that in one day a person can do little else than to walk through them, and give one general gaze of bewildering wonder at the whole scene. And a very long walk it is, I can assure you. At one time, when I set out from the painting rooms, (which are far in the interior of the buildings,) with a party of friends, intending to go out, in order to go home, we walked steadily on at our ordinary pace, without stopping, or deviating from our way, and we found that it took us twenty minutes to get out to our carriage!

In addition to these visits made during the day, small parties are sometimes formed to visit the galleries of statuary by night. It is found that the illumination of a torch, by the strong contrasts of light and shade which it produces, brings out the expression of the statues in a very striking manner, so as to produce sometimes a most

Jacob Abbott

wonderful effect.

It is, however, somewhat expensive to exhibit these statues by torch light, partly on account of the cost of the torches, and partly on account of the attendants that are required. The cost is nearly twenty dollars. It is accordingly customary to make up a party, whenever an evening visit to the Vatican is proposed, in order to divide the expense. The number that can see the statues to advantage in these evening visits is from twelve to fifteen. A party of twelve is sufficient to pay the expense at the rate of a scudo and a half for each person.[7]

[Footnote 7: The scudo is the Roman dollar. It is worth considerably more than the American dollar.]

It was such a plan as this that the gentlemen were forming, whose party Mr. George and Rollo were now proposing to join.

The gentlemen had been much pleased with Rollo's appearance and demeanor when he accosted them, and they were now still more pleased, when they saw Mr. George, to find that he was a young gentleman, of about their own age, and that he was so prepossessing in his countenance and in his air and manner. Mr. George readily agreed to join the party. They asked him if he knew of any body else that he thought would like to go. He inquired whether there were to be any ladies in the party. They said that there were to be several. "Then," said Mr. George, "I will be responsible for the twelfth place. I am quite sure that I can find some person that would like to go.

"And suppose I find more than one?" said Mr. George.

"That will do no harm," replied the gentlemen. "We can have from twelve to fifteen in the party."

"Then I will take the three places," said Mr. George, "and I will pay my proportion now. Which of you gentlemen acts as treasurer?"

One of the three gentlemen said that he had undertaken to collect and pay over the money, but he added that it was not necessary for Mr. George to pay at that time. Mr. George, however, preferred to do so, and he accordingly took out his purse and paid his four scudi and a half, which was the amount due for three persons. The gentlemen seemed to be quite pleased to find that their party was thus made up, and they told Mr. George that since he had taken and paid for the three remaining places, he might bring with him any number of persons that he pleased, so long as he did not make the party more than fifteen in all. It was agreed, too, that the party was to rendezvous that evening, at eight o'clock, at the foot of the grand staircase, leading from the portico of St. Peter's up to the principal court of the Vatican.

Mr. George, as soon as he went home, sent Rollo to Mrs. Beekman's room to inform her of the proposed party, and to ask her if she would like to join it.

"And may I invite Allie too?" asked Rollo.

"Yes," said Mr. George, "and Charles. Though I don't think they will wish to go, for such children generally feel very little interest in statues."

It is true that young persons, like Charles and Allie, generally feel little interest in sculptures and statuary; but, on the other hand, they feel a very great interest in torch light, and both Charles and Allie were exceedingly eager to join the party. It was finally agreed that all three should go. It was arranged that Mr. George and Rollo were to call for them at seven o'clock. Mr. Beekman was engaged to dine that evening with a party of gentlemen, and so he was left out of the account altogether.

At seven o'clock, accordingly, Mr. George and Rollo called at Mrs. Beekman's rooms, and a few minutes afterwards they all went together down to the door of the hotel, where Mr. George beckoned to the coachman of one of the carriages that stood in the square.

The whole party entered the carriage, after Mr. George had made his bargain with the coachman, and immediately set off. They rode for some distance along a pretty straight road, and then came to a bridge, which was opposite to a great round castle. They went over this bridge, and then turning to the left, under the walls of the castle, they went on towards the Vatican.

"We shall arrive there some time before the hour," said Mr. George; "but I thought it was better to be too early than too late "

"Yes," replied Mrs. Beekman, "we can amuse ourselves half an hour in rambling about the colonnades and porticos of St. Peter's."

In front of St. Peter's there is an immense area, enclosed on each side by a magnificent semicircular colonnade. There are four rows of lofty columns in this colonnade, with a carriage way in the centre between them. The space enclosed between these colonnades is called the *piazza*,[A] and it is adorned with fountains and colossal statues, and on days of public festivities and celebrations, it is filled with an immense concourse of people. It is large enough to contain a great many thousands.

[8][Footnote 8: A Pronounced *piatza*.]

When Mr. George and his party arrived, they dismissed the carriage and began to walk to and fro under the colonnade and about the piazza. The time passed away very rapidly; and at length, a few minutes before eight, the other carriages began to come. All the persons who belonged to the party were anxious to arrive in time, for they were afraid that, if they were too late, the others would have gone into the Vatican, where, the building being so immense, it might be very difficult to find them.

Accordingly, before the clock struck eight, all the party were assembled at the entrance door.

The entrance opened from a vast covered gallery, which formed one of the approaches to St. Peter's, between the end of the colonnade and the main front of the building. There were several Swiss sentinels on guard here. They were dressed in what seemed to Rollo a very fantastic garb. In a few minutes the men who were to accompany the party through the galleries appeared. One of them carried a great number of very long candles under his arm. Another had a long pole with a socket at the top of it, and a semicircular screen of tin on one side, to screen the light of the candles from the eyes of the visitors, and to throw it upon the statues. When all was ready, these torch bearers moved on, and were followed by the whole party up the great staircase which led to the galleries of the Vatican.

After going upward and onward for some time, they came at length to the entrance of one of the long galleries of sculpture. Here the torch bearers stopped and began to prepare their torches. They cut the long candles in two, so as to make pieces about eighteen inches long. Taking six or eight of these pieces, they placed them together like a bundle of sticks, and tied them, and then crowded the ends together into the socket upon the end of the pole. This socket was made large enough to receive them. They then lighted the wicks, and thus they had a large number of candles all burning together as one.

The screen, which I have already spoken of, covered this blaze of light upon one side, so as to keep it from shining upon the faces of the company.

Thus provided the torch bearers went on, and the company followed them. Of course, there is only time in the two hours usually appropriated to this exhibition to show a comparatively small number of the statues. The torch bearers accordingly selected such as they thought were most important to be seen, and they passed rapidly on from one to another of these, omitting all the others. When they approached a statue which they were going to exhibit, they would hold the torch up near the face of it in such a manner as to throw a strong light upon the features, and so bring out the expression in a striking manner. The screen shielded the eyes of the company from the direct rays of the flame, and yet there was sufficient light reflected from the marble walls of the gallery, and from the beautiful white surfaces of the statues arranged along them, to enable the company to discern each other very distinctly, and to see all the objects around them.

The company passed in this manner through one of the long galleries, stopping here and there to look at the great masterpieces of ancient art, and then they entered into a series of comparatively smaller chambers and halls. Rollo was exceedingly interested in the exhibition, and in all the attendant circumstances of it; but he could not tell whether Allie was pleased or not. She seemed bewildered and struck dumb with amazement at the strange aspect of the scenes and spectacles which were continually presented to view. The immense extent and the gorgeous magnificence of the galleries and halls, the countless multitude of statues, and the almost spectral appearance which they assumed when the torch bearers threw the bright light of the torch upon their cold marble faces, all impressed her with a solemn awe, which seemed so entirely to subdue and silence her, that Rollo could not tell how she felt, or what she thought of the strange spectacle which he had brought her to see.

After about an hour, the first set of candles that had been put into the socket of the torch pole were burned down, and then the torch bearers supplied their places with another set formed by the remaining halves of the candles which they had cut in two. These lasted another hour. By that time the company had seen all the most striking and celebrated statues in the principal halls and galleries. They had been making a sort of circuit through the palace in passing through these rooms, and now came out very near the entrance door, where they had come in. Here the torch bearers left them, and went away with their apparatus to the part of the building where they belonged, while the company, descending the grand staircase, came out into one of the porticos of the church, and issuing from the portico they found carriages in waiting upon the piazza, and ready to convey them home. Mr. George and his party reached their hotel about nine o'clock, all very much pleased with the spectacle which they had witnessed.

Jacob Abbott

CHAPTER XI

CONCLUSION

Rollo was so much pleased with his torch light visit to the Vatican, and he found, moreover, on talking with Charles and Allie about it the next day, so much evidence of their having been greatly pleased with it, that he planned, a few days afterwards, a torch light visit to the Coliseum. It is very common to make moonlight visits to the Coliseum, but Rollo thought a torch light view of the majestic old ruin would be better. On proposing his plan to his uncle, Mr. George said that he had no objection to it if Rollo would make all the arrangements. He did not know any thing about it himself, he said.

Rollo said he had no doubt that he could arrange it, with the help of a commissioner.

So Rollo looked out a good commissioner, and the commissioner arranged the plan. I have not space to describe this visit fully, but must pass on to the conclusion of the book. I will only say that the torches which were employed on this occasion, were different from those employed in the exhibition of the statues in the Vatican, being more like those used by firemen in America. There were also more of them in number, the commissioner having provided four. With these torch bearers to light their way, Rollo's party explored the Coliseum in every part, and they found that the grandeur and sublimity of the immense corridors and vast vaulted passages of the ruin were greatly enhanced by the solemnity of the night, and by the flickering glare of the torches, shining upon the massive piers, and into the dark recesses of the ruin.

I do not know how many more torch light visits to wonderful places in Rome Rollo would have planned, had not the time arrived when Mr. George thought it was necessary for them to go back to France.

"It is getting late in the season," said Mr. George, "and every body is leaving Rome. I don't think it is safe for us to remain much longer here ourselves, on account of the fever."

Rome is extremely unhealthy in the summer months; and in the environs there is a very wide tract of country which is almost entirely uninhabitable all the year round, on account of the prevalence of fever.

"Very well," said Rollo, "we will go whenever you please."

"We must take our places in the steamer and in the diligences several days beforehand," said Mr. George. "We will go to the steamboat office to-day."

There are several lines of steamers that go from Rome to Marseilles, which is the port of landing for travellers going to France and England. Some of these steamers go "direct" across the sea, while others coast along the shore, sailing at night, and stopping during the day at the large towns on the route. The first night they go to Leghorn, the second to Genoa, and the third to Marseilles. At first Mr. George thought that he would take one of these coasting steamers; but he finally concluded to go "direct."

"It would be very pleasant," said he to Rollo, "for us to stop at those towns, and ramble about during the day, and then in the evening set sail again, provided we could be at liberty to land at our pleasure, to ramble about unmolested wherever we wished to go, as we can do in America."

"And can't we do so?" asked Rollo.

"No," said Mr. George. "In the first place we must have our passports stamped here for all the places that we wish to visit, and that will cause us here a great deal of trouble, and not a little expense. Then to land we must have our passports all examined again, and stamped, and there will be more money to pay; and likely as not we should be detained half the morning in getting through all these formalities, and so our time would be passed in fruitless vexation instead of pleasure. Then, when at last we were free, and began our rambles, we should be beset by beggars every where, and have no peace."

"What a foolish plan it is to plague travellers so much with all these ceremonies about passports!" said Rollo.

"I am not certain that it is foolish for such governments as these," replied Mr. George. "You see, they are governments of force, maintained over the people against their will, by means of military power. The people at large hate the government, and are all the time plotting to destroy it; and if the plotters were allowed to go freely to and fro all over the country, they would be able to organize their plans, and general insurrections would be arranged, and the governments might thus be overthrown. By allowing nobody to travel without a passport, stating who he is, and where he came from, and where he is going, the government keep every thing under their control."

"But I think the governments *ought* to be overthrown," said Rollo, "and better governments, such as the people would like, set up in their places."

"So do I," said Mr. George; "but it is not surprising that the governors themselves of these countries don't think so. They wish to retain their stations and their power, whether the people like it or not; and the passport system is a very cunning contrivance to help them do it. And then, besides, they have a very good pretext for keeping up the system."

"What is their pretext?" asked Rollo.

"They pretend that the object is to assist them in stopping and arresting robbers, and murderers, and other criminals who attempt to escape from one part of the country to another after committing their crimes. And the system is sometimes useful in this way, I have no doubt; though these criminals can often elude the authorities by procuring false passports."

"And the plotters against the government, too, I suppose," said Rollo.

"Yes," said Mr. George, "sometimes."

This conversation took place while Mr. George and Rollo were walking towards the steamboat office, to take their passages to Marseilles.

They arrived at the office. The clerk answered their

inquiries in respect to the steamer with great politeness. The conversation was in the French language. He told them that the steamer started from Naples every evening, and that it stopped in the morning about eight o'clock at Civita Vecchia[9] to take in the passengers from Rome. It was necessary for the passengers to go from Rome to Civita Vecchia by diligence, or by post, or with a vetturino.

[Footnote 9: Pronounced *Tchivita Vekkia*.]

"Then there are no carriages from your office," said Mr. George.

"No, sir," replied the clerk. "We take the passengers at Civita Vecchia. They find their own conveyances there."

"Very well," said Mr. George. "I will take two berths in the steamer for Thursday morning. Can I see a plan of the steamer so as to select the berths?"

"No, sir," said the clerk, "we have no plan of the steamer. And besides, we cannot positively promise you any berths. It depends upon how many passengers there are from Naples The passengers from Rome take the berths that are left vacant. They take them in the order in which they take passage here."

"Are there many that have taken passage before us?" asked Mr. George.

"No, sir," said the clerk, "only two. Your numbers are 3 and 4."

"Then, if there are more than two berths that are not occupied by the Naples passengers, we can have them?"

"Yes, sir," said the clerk.

"And suppose there are not more than two," asked Rollo, "what shall we do then?"

"Why, then you will have sofas or cots," said the clerk.

"O, that will do just as well," said Rollo. "I would as lief have a sofa or a cot as a berth."

So Mr. George paid the money, and took tickets numbers 3 and 4, and then, having inquired the way to the diligence office, they bade the clerk good morning, and went away.

"And now," said Mr. George, "we must go directly to the diligence office, and secure our places for Civita Vecchia. If we put it off, the places might all be taken, and then we should lose the passage money we have paid for the steamer."

"Would not they pay us back again?" asked Rollo.

"I am afraid not," said Mr. George. "But I think we are in season, for it is now Tuesday, and we do not sail till Thursday."

On entering the diligence office, Mr. George saw one or two clerks standing behind a counter. They seemed busy talking with persons who had come in to engage places, and entering their names in great books. As soon as one of the clerks was at liberty Mr. George accosted him, saying that he wished to get two places in the diligence for Civita Vecchia on Wednesday.

The clerk looked at the book, and said that all the places

were taken for Wednesday, except one.

"That's bad,' said Mr. George. "We shall have to go down on Tuesday, then, and stay a day at Civita Vecchia. Are there any places for Tuesday?"

The clerk looked, and said that every place for Tuesday was engaged.

"But there is a coach on Wednesday night," he added, "that arrives at Civita Vecchia in the morning in time for the steamer."

Then turning over to another place in his book, he looked at the list of names, and then told Mr. George that there was only one vacant place for Wednesday night.

"Dear me, Rollo!" said Mr. George, "how unfortunate! We ought to have attended to this business before."

"I'll tell you what we can do," said Rollo. "One of us can go on Wednesday morning, and the other wait here and come on in the night."

"That is the only thing that we *can* do," said Mr. George, "unless we hire a carriage to ourselves, and that would be expensive. Should you dare to go alone?"

"O, yes, indeed," said Rollo.

"But remember," said Mr. George, "that all the people will be speaking Italian. You will have to ride among them like a deaf and dumb boy."

"Never mind that," said Rollo. "Deaf and dumb boys get along in travelling very well. Besides, I am almost sure that there will be somebody in the diligence that can speak French or English."

"And which would you rather do," asked Mr. George, "go in the morning or in the evening? If you go in the morning coach, you will have to set out very early, before it is light, and then stay at Civita Vecchia, in a strange hotel, alone, all night. If you go in the evening, you can remain here, where you are acquainted, all day; but then you will have to ride alone in the night."

"I would rather go in the morning coach," said Rollo.

"Very well," said Mr. George. "That's what we'll do."

This conversation between Mr. George and Rollo had been carried on in English; but now Mr. George turned to the clerk, and said in French that he would take the two places that were left, one in the morning coach and one in the evening coach of Wednesday. The place in the morning coach was upon the banquette. The one in the evening coach was in the coupe. Mr. George had scarcely uttered the words by which he engaged the seats, before two gentlemen came in in a hurried manner to ask for seats in the diligence for Wednesday. The clerk told them that the last of them had just been engaged.

When Wednesday morning came, Rollo was awakened by the porter of the hotel knocking at his door before it was light. He got up, and opened the door a little way, and took in the candles which the porter handed to him. Mr. George had intended to get up too, and go with Rollo to the office; but Rollo particularly desired that he should not do so.

"I have nothing to carry," said he, "but my little valise,

and the porter will go with me to take that, and to see me safe through the streets. So that it is not at all necessary for you to go, and I would much rather not have you go."

Mr. George perceived that Rollo felt a pride in taking care of himself on this occasion, and so he yielded to this request, and remained in his bed. If he had not been convinced that Rollo would be perfectly safe under the porter's care. he would of course have insisted on going himself. Rollo was soon dressed, and then going to his uncle's bedside, he shook hands with him, and bade him good by.

"I shall be looking out for you at the diligence office in Civita Vecchia," said he, "when the diligence arrives to-morrow morning."

So saying, he took his candle in one hand and his valise in the other, and sallied forth into the long corridor of the hotel. He had to walk a a great distance along this corridor, passing a great many doors, with a pair of boots or shoes before each of them, before he reached the head of the staircase. He descended the staircase, and at the bottom of it found the porter waiting for him. The porter had another candle, which was upon a table in the hall. He took Rollo's candle, and also the valise, and then unbolted and unlocked the front door. A sleepy-looking boy was ready to lock it again, after Rollo and the porter had gone out.

So they sallied forth into the cool morning air. There were lamps burning in the streets, and in one direction, where there was an opening among the buildings, Rollo could see some faint signs of the dawn in the eastern sky.

The porter could only speak Italian; so he and Rollo

walked along together in silence through the solitary streets. They soon arrived at the diligence office, where there was a bright light of lanterns, and a bustle of people coming and going, and of postilions bringing out horses. The diligence was all ready before the door. The baggage, which had been brought for the purpose the night before, was all loaded. Rollo paid the porter, and then climbed up to his place on the banquette. The horses were soon harnessed in, and the diligence set off; but there were several stoppages necessary at police stations and passport offices before the journey was fairly commenced, so that the sun was rising when Rollo took his final leave of Rome.

He had a very pleasant journey across the country, and arrived at Civita Vecchia about three o'clock. As he descended from the coach, a pleasant-looking man, in a sort of official costume, accosted him, asking him if he was going to Leghorn in the steamer that afternoon. The man spoke in English, though with a foreign accent.

"No," said Rollo; "I am going to Marseilles to-morrow morning."

"Ah! Then you go to the hotel," said the man. "This porter will take your valise, and show you the way."

So saying, the man, who was a commissioner of the hotel, put Rollo under the charge of a porter, who conducted him to a large and very substantial-looking hotel near by. Rollo ascended by a flight of stone stairs into the second story of the hotel, and there engaged a room for the night, and ordered dinner. He had a very good dinner, all by himself, in a great dining room with long tables in it, where there were at the same time several other persons and parties dining. After dinner he went out to ramble

Jacob Abbott

about the town. He was surprised at the massive masonry of the piers, and breakwaters, and forts, that lined the shores, and at the number of vessels and steamers in the basin. He returned to the hotel in good season, and amused himself there till nine o'clock observing the different parties of travellers that were continually coming and going.

The next morning he watched for the diligence from a piazza on the second story of the hotel—the diligence office being at the next door. The diligence arrived at the proper time, and Rollo called out to his uncle George when he saw him getting out from the coupe. This was at seven o'clock; at eight Mr. George and Rollo embarked, with a great many others, in a small boat, to go on board the steamer, and at half past eight the paddles of the steamer began to revolve, and to bear them rapidly away from the shores of Italy out over the blue waters of the Mediterranean, on the route to Marseilles.

ABOUT THE AUTHOR

Jacob Abbott (November 14, 1803–October 31, 1879) was an American writer of children's books.

Abbott was born at Hallowell, Maine. He graduated from Bowdoin College in 1820; studied at Andover Theological Seminary in 1821, 1822, and 1824; was tutor in 1824-1825, and from 1825 to 1829 was professor of mathematics and natural philosophy at Amherst College; was licensed to preach by the Hampshire Association in 1826; founded the Mount Vernon School for Young Ladies in Boston in 1829, and was principal of it in 1829-1833; was pastor of Eliot Congregational Church (which he founded), at Roxbury, Massachusetts in 1834-1835; and was, with his brothers, a founder, and in 1843-1851 a principal of Abbott's Institute, and in 1845-1848 of the Mount Vernon School for boys, in New York City.

He was a prolific author, writing juvenile fiction, brief histories, biographies, religious books for the general reader, and a few works in popular science. He died in Farmington, Maine, where he had spent part of his time after 1839, and where his brother Samuel Phillips Abbott founded the Abbott School.

His Rollo Books, such as Rollo at Work, Rollo at Play, Rollo in Europe, etc., are the best known of his writings, having as their chief characters a representative boy and his associates. His brothers, John Stevens Cabot Abbott and Gorham Dummer Abbott, were also authors.

Other books by this author

Cleopatra

History of King Charles The Second of England

Mary Erskine

Peter the Great

Rollo In Holland

Rollo In Paris

Choose from Thousands of 1stWorldLibrary Classics By

A. M. Barnard
Ada Leverson
Adolphus William Ward
Aesop
Agatha Christie
Alexander Aaronsohn
Alexander Kielland
Alexandre Dumas
Alfred Gatty
Alfred Ollivant
Alice Duer Miller
Alice Turner Curtis
Alice Dunbar
Allen Chapman
Alleyne Ireland
Ambrose Bierce
Amelia E. Barr
Amory H. Bradford
Andrew Lang
Andrew McFarland Davis
Andy Adams
Angela Brazil
Anna Alice Chapin
Anna Sewell
Annie Besant
Annie Hamilton Donnell
Annie Payson Call
Annie Roe Carr
Annonaymous
Anton Chekhov
Archibald Lee Fletcher
Arnold Bennett
Arthur C. Benson
Arthur Conan Doyle
Arthur M. Winfield
Arthur Ransome
Arthur Schnitzler
Arthur Train
Atticus
B.H. Baden-Powell
B. M. Bower
B. C. Chatterjee
Baroness Emmuska Orczy
Baroness Orczy
Basil King
Bayard Taylor
Ben Macomber
Bertha Muzzy Bower
Bjornstjerne Bjornson

Booth Tarkington
Boyd Cable
Bram Stoker
C. Collodi
C. E. Orr
C. M. Ingleby
Carolyn Wells
Catherine Parr Traill
Charles A. Eastman
Charles Amory Beach
Charles Dickens
Charles Dudley Warner
Charles Farrar Browne
Charles Ives
Charles Kingsley
Charles Klein
Charles Hanson Towne
Charles Lathrop Pack
Charles Romyn Dake
Charles Whibley
Charles Willing Beale
Charlotte M. Braeme
Charlotte M. Yonge
Charlotte Perkins Stetson
Clair W. Hayes
Clarence Day Jr.
Clarence E. Mulford
Clemence Housman
Confucius
Coningsby Dawson
Cornelis DeWitt Wilcox
Cyril Burleigh
D. H. Lawrence
Daniel Defoe
David Garnett
Dinah Craik
Don Carlos Janes
Donald Keyhoe
Dorothy Kilner
Dougan Clark
Douglas Fairbanks
E. Nesbit
E. P. Roe
E. Phillips Oppenheim
E. S. Brooks
Earl Barnes
Edgar Rice Burroughs
Edith Van Dyne
Edith Wharton

Edward Everett Hale
Edward J. O'Biren
Edward S. Ellis
Edwin L. Arnold
Eleanor Atkins
Eleanor Hallowell Abbott
Eliot Gregory
Elizabeth Gaskell
Elizabeth McCracken
Elizabeth Von Arnim
Ellem Key
Emerson Hough
Emilie F. Carlen
Emily Bronte
Emily Dickinson
Enid Bagnold
Enilor Macartney Lane
Erasmus W. Jones
Ernie Howard Pie
Ethel May Dell
Ethel Turner
Ethel Watts Mumford
Eugene Sue
Eugenie Foa
Eugene Wood
Eustace Hale Ball
Evelyn Everett-green
Everard Cotes
F. H. Cheley
F. J. Cross
F. Marion Crawford
Fannie E. Newberry
Federick Austin Ogg
Ferdinand Ossendowski
Fergus Hume
Florence A. Kilpatrick
Fremont B. Deering
Francis Bacon
Francis Darwin
Frances Hodgson Burnett
Frances Parkinson Keyes
Frank Gee Patchin
Frank Harris
Frank Jewett Mather
Frank L. Packard
Frank V. Webster
Frederic Stewart Isham
Frederick Trevor Hill
Frederick Winslow Taylor

Friedrich Kerst
Friedrich Nietzsche
Fyodor Dostoyevsky
G.A. Henty
G.K. Chesterton
Gabrielle E. Jackson
Garrett P. Serviss
Gaston Leroux
George A. Warren
George Ade
Geroge Bernard Shaw
George Cary Eggleston
George Durston
George Ebers
George Eliot
George Gissing
George MacDonald
George Meredith
George Orwell
George Sylvester Viereck
George Tucker
George W. Cable
George Wharton James
Gertrude Atherton
Gordon Cassely
Grace E. King
Grace Gallatin
Grace Greenwood
Grant Allen
Guillermo A. Sherwell
Gulielma Zollinger
Gustav Flaubert
H. A. Cody
H. B. Irving
H. C. Bailey
H. G. Wells
H. H. Munro
H. Irving Hancock
H. R. Naylor
H. Rider Haggard
H. W. C. Davis
Haldeman Julius
Hall Caine
Hamilton Wright Mabie
Hans Christian Andersen
Harold Avery
Harold McGrath
Harriet Beecher Stowe
Harry Castlemon
Harry Coghill
Harry Houidini

Hayden Carruth
Helent Hunt Jackson
Helen Nicolay
Hendrik Conscience
Hendy David Thoreau
Henri Barbusse
Henrik Ibsen
Henry Adams
Henry Ford
Henry Frost
Henry James
Henry Jones Ford
Henry Seton Merriman
Henry W Longfellow
Herbert A. Giles
Herbert Carter
Herbert N. Casson
Herman Hesse
Hildegard G. Frey
Homer
Honore De Balzac
Horace B. Day
Horace Walpole
Horatio Alger Jr.
Howard Pyle
Howard R. Garis
Hugh Lofting
Hugh Walpole
Humphry Ward
Ian Maclaren
Inez Haynes Gillmore
Irving Bacheller
Isabel Cecilia Williams
Isabel Hornibrook
Israel Abrahams
Ivan Turgenev
J. G.Austin
J. Henri Fabre
J. M. Barrie
J. M. Walsh
J. Macdonald Oxley
J. R. Miller
J. S. Fletcher
J. S. Knowles
J. Storer Clouston
J. W. Duffield
Jack London
Jacob Abbott
James Allen
James Andrews
James Baldwin

James Branch Cabell
James DeMille
James Joyce
James Lane Allen
James Lane Allen
James Oliver Curwood
James Oppenheim
James Otis
James R. Driscoll
Jane Abbott
Jane Austen
Jane L. Stewart
Janet Aldridge
Jens Peter Jacobsen
Jerome K. Jerome
Jessie Graham Flower
John Buchan
John Burroughs
John Cournos
John F. Kennedy
John Gay
John Glasworthy
John Habberton
John Joy Bell
John Kendrick Bangs
John Milton
John Philip Sousa
John Taintor Foote
Jonas Lauritz Idemil Lie
Jonathan Swift
Joseph A. Altsheler
Joseph Carey
Joseph Conrad
Joseph E. Badger Jr
Joseph Hergesheimer
Joseph Jacobs
Jules Vernes
Julian Hawthrone
Julie A Lippmann
Justin Huntly McCarthy
Kakuzo Okakura
Karle Wilson Baker
Kate Chopin
Kenneth Grahame
Kenneth McGaffey
Kate Langley Bosher
Kate Langley Bosher
Katherine Cecil Thurston
Katherine Stokes
L. A. Abbot
L. T. Meade

L. Frank Baum
Latta Griswold
Laura Dent Crane
Laura Lee Hope
Laurence Housman
Lawrence Beasley
Leo Tolstoy
Leonid Andreyev
Lewis Carroll
Lewis Sperry Chafer
Lilian Bell
Lloyd Osbourne
Louis Hughes
Louis Joseph Vance
Louis Tracy
Louisa May Alcott
Lucy Fitch Perkins
Lucy Maud Montgomery
Luther Benson
Lydia Miller Middleton
Lyndon Orr
M. Corvus
M. H. Adams
Margaret E. Sangster
Margret Howth
Margaret Vandercook
Margaret W. Hungerford
Margret Penrose
Maria Edgeworth
Maria Thompson Daviess
Mariano Azuela
Marion Polk Angellotti
Mark Overton
Mark Twain
Mary Austin
Mary Catherine Crowley
Mary Cole
Mary Hastings Bradley
Mary Roberts Rinehart
Mary Rowlandson
M. Wollstonecraft Shelley
Maud Lindsay
Max Beerbohm
Myra Kelly
Nathaniel Hawthrone
Nicolo Machiavelli
O. F. Walton
Oscar Wilde
Owen Johnson
P.G. Wodehouse
Paul and Mabel Thorne

Paul G. Tomlinson
Paul Severing
Percy Brebner
Percy Keese Fitzhugh
Peter B. Kyne
Plato
Quincy Allen
R. Derby Holmes
R. L. Stevenson
R. S. Ball
Rabindranath Tagore
Rahul Alvares
Ralph Bonehill
Ralph Henry Barbour
Ralph Victor
Ralph Waldo Emmerson
Rene Descartes
Ray Cummings
Rex Beach
Rex E. Beach
Richard Harding Davis
Richard Jefferies
Richard Le Gallienne
Robert Barr
Robert Frost
Robert Gordon Anderson
Robert L. Drake
Robert Lansing
Robert Lynd
Robert Michael Ballantyne
Robert W. Chambers
Rosa Nouchette Carey
Rudyard Kipling
Saint Augustine
Samuel B. Allison
Samuel Hopkins Adams
Sarah Bernhardt
Sarah C. Hallowell
Selma Lagerlof
Sherwood Anderson
Sigmund Freud
Standish O'Grady
Stanley Weyman
Stella Benson
Stella M. Francis
Stephen Crane
Stewart Edward White
Stijn Streuvels
Swami Abhedananda
Swami Parmananda
T. S. Ackland

T. S. Arthur
The Princess Der Ling
Thomas A. Janvier
Thomas A Kempis
Thomas Anderton
Thomas Bailey Aldrich
Thomas Bulfinch
Thomas De Quincey
Thomas Dixon
Thomas H. Huxley
Thomas Hardy
Thomas More
Thornton W. Burgess
U. S. Grant
Upton Sinclair
Valentine Williams
Various Authors
Vaughan Kester
Victor Appleton
Victor G. Durham
Victoria Cross
Virginia Woolf
Wadsworth Camp
Walter Camp
Walter Scott
Washington Irving
Wilbur Lawton
Wilkie Collins
Willa Cather
Willard F. Baker
William Dean Howells
William le Queux
W. Makepeace Thackeray
William W. Walter
William Shakespeare
Winston Churchill
Yei Theodora Ozaki
Yogi Ramacharaka
Young E. Allison
Zane Grey

www.ingramcontent.com/pod-product-compliance
Lightning Source LLC
Chambersburg PA
CBHW051825170626
46807CB00003B/1025